COOKING
FOR
CAMPERS

COOKING FOR CAMPERS

Joy Booth

HAMLYN
London · New York · Sydney · Toronto

To my husband who improves with keeping.

Line drawings by David Bryant
Cover photograph by John Lee
Equipment for cover photograph kindly supplied by
Camping Gaz (G.B.) Limited

First published in 1967
This edition published in 1979 by
The Hamlyn Publishing Group Limited
London · New York · Sydney · Toronto
Astronaut House, Feltham, Middlesex, England
© Copyright Joy Booth 1967

ISBN 0 600 32114 2

Printed in Italy

Contents

Introduction

Compiling this book was an exercise in self-indulgence. Not only did it mean cooking, over a period of time, all the food that I like best, but I have ensured that all my favourite recipes are contained in a book small enough to fit into a rucksack!

But I hope, also, that these recipes will be useful to the growing numbers who periodically escape to the simple life as an antidote to our everyday prepackaged world.

Some of the recipes given here are original. Most of them are not. They have been culled gratefully from sources unfortunately too numerous to mention, and adapted where necessary to meet the needs of the camper and the small boat sailor. Although all the recipes in this book can be followed slavishly I shall be well content if some of them fulfil the secondary function of triggering off ideas, since the essence of inspired cookery is constant experimentation.

And when you are cooking away from home, the willingness to improvise will often turn a mediocre meal into a feast. And since like soldiers, campers camp and sailors sail on their stomachs, improvisation may mean the difference between a dull trip and a memorable one.

There are no recipes in this book which require the use of an oven. If you have an oven all things are possible and no special cook-book is necessary. Nor have I given recipes for pressure cookers since high pressure types never stir without them anyway.

With one exception there are no recipes for soups—who wants to fiddle with stockpots under canvas? But it is not difficult to produce something unexpected from the excellent package soups by combining flavours and by the addition of simple garnishes of grated cheese, chopped parsley, croûtons and so on.

It isn't possible to be very exact about cooking times as equipment varies greatly and the weather plays its part. But even in a Force 8 gale it shouldn't be necessary to add more than about ten minutes to the times given.

Equipment

Experienced camp and galley cooks have their own permanent lists of the equipment which is essential to them. Each to his own. But probably absorbent kitchen paper and metal foil are the two articles which every cook includes. I know that I should hate to work without them; kitchen paper because it makes the washing up less unpleasant, and foil for easy improvisation.

When weight is no problem my favourite cooking pot is a very large heavy frying pan with rounded sides and a well-fitting lid. In this I cook braised dishes, curries, risottos, and spaghetti sauce. In fact I use it for almost everything except frying and omelettes, and for these I use a smaller non-stick pan.

Then I take a couple of saucepans—two is usually plenty but if the party is a large one I add a double saucepan. Both my pans are the same size. The lids don't fit too well but metal foil remedies this. A griddle goes as well when I am likely to be cooking over an open fire.

A pressure cooker can also prove to be an invaluable addition to your equipment. By cooking vegetables in the top sections and meat beneath them, you can cook in one pot what would otherwise take several, and do so in a fraction of the time. And it cuts down on the washing up too.

Then I have an ovenglass bowl which is used for salads and for puddings and mixing. It has lugs on each side and these fit neatly over either of my saucepans for steaming or merely heating something through over the potatoes. The jug I take is also ovenglass and if necessary I can use that for steaming a pudding, too. As a bonus it is marked in fluid ounces.

A tray and a chopping board are necessities—one side of the board for bread and one for vegetables and meat. Then of course a really sharp knife with a cork on its point for safe stowage. By the way, if you want to get rid of the taste of onions or garlic from a knife, quickly pass the blade through a flame and it will do the trick miraculously.

I'm lost without a potato peeler which I also use for grating cheese and making dinky little curls of chocolate to decorate simple puddings. Looks quite impressive.

A can opener is essential of course, and a wooden or melamine spatula for the non-stick pan. A fish slice does for the other one. And spoons: wooden, tea, dessert, table and perforated.

9

If we're cooking on bottled gas I take a couple of asbestos mats. I've never yet been able to turn the jet right down to simmering point without putting out the flame. Perhaps you have the knack, in which case you won't need an asbestos mat.

For me, that's about all the essentials. Of course there is a wide choice of modern equipment available for campers— apart from the essential gas or paraffin burners, there are portable ovens, insulated bags and iceboxes and even complete kitchen units with storage racks, larder space and shelves.

The lightweight camper with his gear pared right down to the bare essentials will regard most of this equipment as superfluous. He will eat well with just his Gilwell canteen, and his knife, fork, mug and spoon.

For him, as for all of us who cook away from home, from the canoeist to the caravanner, the advent of plastics has made airtight storage much simpler.

On any camping trip, no matter how short, it is wise to take a basic First Aid kit to cope with any accidents with the cooking, and an insect repellent to protect yourself from the insects which always gather where there is food.

Stores

Quite obviously it is not possible to pack the entire contents of the pantry when the itch to be off gets unbearable. Most likely you'll be within reach of shops for most of the time, anyway. But it's pretty silly to have to buy something like curry powder when there's some deteriorating daily on the pantry shelf at home. And the inclusion of herbs and spices, rice, breadcrumbs, tubed tomato purée, and grated cheese, all of which take up very little space, can help to turn the simplest ingredients into a feast.

I've learnt from bitter experience that on even the most sedate trip the stores MUST include at all times the ingredients of a quickly prepared emergency meal, to cover such eventualities as going aground on a falling tide with nothing in the food locker, or finding all the shops shut because it is Pentecost.

Emergency stores are also useful when you arrive at a fresh camp site after dark and very tired. By the time the tent is pitched there is little energy left for cooking. Our emergency meal for such occasions is sometimes a simple curry made with canned meat, sometimes Cowboys' supper or Camp chilli. Similarly we always carry breakfast biscuits and the makings of drop scones or twists.

As the Irishman said, 'One Man's Meat is another Man's Poison', but WE take all the following on even the shortest expedition:

tea	nutmeg, cinnamon, ginger
sugar	marmalade
coffee	potatoes
bacon	onions
butter	tomatoes, lettuce, cucumber
eggs	fresh fruit
salt	rice
pepper mill	packet soups
squeezy lemon	mint, parsley, marjoram in
tomato purée	closed polythene bag
cornflour	breakfast biscuits
cheese	sweet biscuits
grated cheese	substantial homemade cake
canned milk	breadcrumbs
dried milk	ingredients for the
olive oil	emergency meal
vinegar	

When we are in the fresh air all day we seem to need a higher proportion of carbohydrates than we do at home, and of course dietary needs vary in other ways. If it's very cold a slightly higher fat intake is a good thing, but at sea if the crew are likely to feel queasy until they get their sea legs, fat should be cut right down. If they feel like eating at all it may be sweet things they want or it may be the clean sharp flavours of salads and fruit. There's nothing like the Italian remedy of boiled rice for settling upset stomachs.

Strange water can disturb the digestion, too, and it's wise to pack alkaseltzer and vegetable laxatives.

And talking of water, beware of taps with strange markings or none at all. We once made tea in an unknown boat from a tap clearly marked Whale. It certainly tasted a bit odd and fishy. Afterwards we found that it was instant river water! Fortunately none of the party was ill, but it could have ruined the whole trip at the outset. Nowadays we periodically rinse out all water containers with a weak solution of Milton. But even Milton wouldn't do a great deal for river water.

If we are setting off for more than a night or two we include in addition the following basic stores:

flour (sieved)
rolled oats
oatmeal
curry powder
desiccated coconut
mustard
bicarbonate soda
baking powder
cocoa
icing sugar
brown sugar
bouillon cubes
Worcestershire sauce
sauce mixes

cooked pastry shells
fruit loaf
dried herbs
dehydrated potato
dried fruit
jam
sponge biscuits
cans of: —
    fruit
    cream
    tomatoes
    meat
    fish
    frankfurters
    pork sausages

Plastic containers are obtainable in all shapes and sizes, but when space is limited we take square ones, and I bake square cakes. And I vary the sizes of the pastry shells if I take more than one, so that they nest one inside another.

Without a refrigerator hot weather storage of perishables can be tricky. Meat and fats can travel in wide mouthed vacuum jars, with ice. Or if it isn't TOO hot, an alternative is to put them in plastic containers and sling them in string bags in a draughty spot, or cool them in a mountain stream or over the shady side of the boat.

Milk can also go into vacuum flasks, or under an evaporating milk cooler. Such a cooler can be improvised by placing the container in a bowl of water and draping a teacloth over it with its ends in the water. Heat needed for evaporation is drawn from the milk.

Butter can be treated in the same way, and salt butter keeps better than unsalted.

Oil is most convenient for frying in hot weather (that is, if you WANT to fry in the heat).

I should never try to keep offal or fish overnight without a refrigerator or icebox, and I wouldn't really be very happy about red meat either, although marinating it improves its chances. If in the slightest doubt, don't!

If you aren't able to buy freshly just before the meal, play safe and use tins. You will find recipes for dishes using canned meat or fish on page 141 onwards.

Sailors will know the trick of marking all their canned goods with a simple code and then stripping off the labels before stowage. Soggy paper in the bilge pump doesn't improve the temper and it's dangerous.

Guessing the contents of an unlabelled can is hilarious at first but palls after five successive cans of peas have been opened in search of apricots. Use a wax crayon for marking—it won't dissolve.

Tablespoon measures

approximate number of level tablespoons to the ounce

rice	2
oatmeal	2
rolled oats	4
flour (unsifted)	2 (scant)
flour (sifted)	3
cornflour	3
shredded suet	3
grated cheese	4
breadcrumbs (fine)	3 (scant)
breadcrumbs (coarse)	4 (scant)
semolina	$2\frac{1}{2}$
cocoa	3
sugar	2
sultanas	2
raisins	2
currants	2
desiccated coconut	4
chopped nuts	4
butter	2 (smoothed off)
golden syrup or treacle	1

Miscellaneous

1 medium-sized lemon	yields 4 tablespoons juice
1 medium-sized orange	yields $\frac{1}{8}$ pint juice
8 lumps of sugar	equals 1 oz.

Cooking
on one burner

The easiest way to produce a complete meal on one burner is to cook a main dish that needs only one pan, such as a risotto or a Sea pie.

But the one-burner cook is by no means restricted to this type of cookery. With a little juggling a great variety of meals can be produced. For instance, anything that includes a sauce is possible—the sauce can be prepared first, covered if it is likely to form a skin, and quickly heated through when the main part of the meal has been cooked.

A steamer is useful. Cans can be put in a steamer with their lids off and the whole thing put on top of the potato saucepan, and everything will be ready about the same time. A double saucepan is equally useful.

A variety of ingredients can be cooked quite separately in one saucepan if each is individually wrapped in metal foil and they are all plunged into boiling water. For instance you could have one parcel of potatoes, another of chopped onion and carrot, each with seasoning and a knob of butter, and frankfurters in a third parcel. Waiting in a separate pan could be a sauce ready to be whipped on to the burner as soon as the sausages and vegetables are cooked.

And of course exactly the same sort of thing can be done with a pressure cooker.

Recipes for main dishes which are easy to cook on one burner

Lightweight camping

The lightweight camper—and to a lesser extent the canoeist—will plan his meals in detail before he leaves home. He doesn't want to carry a store of backbreaking canned foods, but the exact ingredients for satisfying and well balanced meals.

Accelerated freeze dried foods are a great help to the lightweight man. He can, if he wishes, use them exclusively for his main meals—the choice is quite wide. AFD meals are reliable although sometimes the portions are not very generous. The real featherweight man can even cook on his playing-card-sized stove from a special carton of rations measuring 10 × 4 × 2 inches, which includes not only completely balanced food for 2 days but a book of matches and a wooden spatula as well. There's glory for you!

When you think of the cost of packaging and the convenience you wouldn't expect any of these wonder foods to be cheap. You pays your money and you takes your choice.

Aside from ready prepared foods, there are one or two other things that weigh very little that I would always include. Such things as dried herbs, grated cheese, and of course salt and pepper. And curry powder and spices and the last quarter of a tube of tomato purée if the menu called for them. Each item can travel in its own firmly closed polythene bag. Instant potato is useful where weight is important. So is rice for one pan meals—a good risotto is probably the lightweight camper's easiest substantial meal, with bacon and mushroom kebabs served with Swel or Surprise peas a close runner up for the camp fire cook.

Bacon, cheese and eggs can supply necessary protein and weigh less than cans of meat and fish. And if the bacon is fairly fat there will be no need to take additional fat for frying. Eggs need careful packing, but a plastic 2-egg container can be bought very cheaply and it also has space for salt. The whole thing weighs 2 oz. An alternative is to take a packet of Omelet mix. The flavour is good although the texture is more like that of scrambled egg than of omelette.

With the aid of tea bags it is possible to make tea direct in the mug, providing that it is made of metal.

Walkers, cyclists and canoeists burn up a lot of energy and need a fairly high carbohydrate intake. Weight for weight, a slab of home made fruit cake is pretty good. Chocolate, Kendal mint cake, dried fruit and glucose sweets go down well in the open air, too. And crisp apples are thirst quenching and worth their weight.

Surprising things come in tubes nowadays. Besides tomato purée there is mustard, condensed milk and jam—they are all useful in camp or afloat, and keep fresh almost indefinitely.

The following recipes will be useful to the lightweight camper:

The open fire

Eating beneath the stars around a camp fire is one of the great simple pleasures of life. Ideally the day should have been hot—too hot to eat—the company should be congenial, the food delectable.

22

On organised camp sites nowadays it is seldom possible to light an open fire, but even in this crowded island there ARE places where it can be done. Lone campers have their own secret places, and dinghy sailors know the delights of barbecues on lonely beaches. Beware of stony shingly beaches, though. When flints get hot they fly around dangerously.

If you are camping on a farmer's land you will of course have to get permission before you can light a fire. Convince him that you will be careful and that it will be difficult to find traces of your fire after you have left, and he will probably give you permission. Understandably, he may be reluctant in very dry windy weather, especially if your camp site is near to woods or dry gorse.

To build a cooking fire in a meadow, first of all cut a turf about a yard square and 3-inches thick. Either roll it back or remove it completely. If you are staying for more than one night, water the turf well from time to time. Then, on striking camp, you can level the ground and replace the turf, treading it down and watering it well with the last of the contents of the water carrier.

Soak any remaining charred sticks, to be on the safe side, and conceal them in the hedge bottom. Later, when the yellow square in the grass where your tent has stood has turned to green again, the only sign of your recent occupation should be the crossed sticks laid over your neatly filled grease and rubbish pit.

Make sure that you have plenty of wood before lighting the fire—about twice as much as you think you will need. Conifers are good for starting but they burn away very quickly and the hard woods are best for cooking. Ash, beech and oak burn well with little smoke, and apple and cherry are good and fragrant. Elm, willow and alder are all poor burners. Elder burns well but gives off the most ghastly smoke.

Unless the weather has been very dry, wood found lying on the ground will probably be damp and unsuitable for starting the fire. But there will be some small dead branches still on the trees to use at first. And keep a little of this precious dry stuff under cover for starting tomorrow's fire.

Making a wigwam of small dry sticks is probably the easiest way of getting the fire going. The centre is filled with dry grass or bracken—the faint-hearted can use paper—and set alight on the windward side. Gradually as the flames take hold add larger and larger pieces of wood. But this sort of fire, although it will boil your kettle, isn't yet ready for cooking.

The blaze must die down to hot embers before you start to cook, and preferably be contained between 2 logs to hold the pots and pans. And if you want to scramble eggs or cook something else which needs gentle heat, just rake out a few embers to one side and cook on these. When by daylight they look quite grey and practically out the heat should be about right.

Now when you are ready to start cooking Fingal's Law comes into operation.

Canoeists know all about Fingal's Law. It's one which says that if you drop a piece of bread and butter it will fall butter side down—except when you drop a piece of bread and butter to demonstrate the law, when it will fall butter side up!

So when you are ready to start cooking and have taken careful note of the prevailing wind, have set out all your food and utensils on the windward side of the fire, and are squatting on your haunches at the ready, without a doubt the wind will change and you will have to move round to the other side.

I can't think, offhand, of many things that cannot be cooked on a camp fire—you can even roast if you are clever enough to include in your party someone who can improvise a reflector oven or a Dutch oven. With a salamander you can grill as well. Most dishes that can be left alone to cook don't suffer if the heat source fluctuates a bit. The pineapple pan pudding, see page 209, does need a very low, steady heat, though, and I don't think I'd try this one on a open fire.

Steamed puddings however, see page 219, don't come to any harm if they are cooked for longer than the specified time, and just as long as the water doesn't go off the boil they are fine.

Hay box cookery

If you are running a standing camp from which you set off each day, an old-fashioned hay box is a useful thing to have. It's almost as good as a timer at home and you can arrange to have a hot meal ready for your return to camp in the evening.

You will need a wooden box which will take your largest saucepan or billycan with 3 or 4-inches to spare all the way round. Seal off any cracks in the box with sticky tape and line the whole thing with several thicknesses of newspaper. Then stuff hay into the box, packing it as tightly as possible— and I do mean tightly—around the cooking pot you intend to use. Fix a pad of hay to the lid, which must fit very snugly indeed.

The food must be brought to boiling point in the cooking pot, the pot transferred to the hay box for a little while, then brought to the boil again.

It can then be sealed up in the haybox and left to cook away on its own, but it will take 3 or 4 times as long as if it were on a burner.

If you want to find your breakfast porridge ready for you when you get up, cook it for 5 minutes and put it in the hay box before you go to bed.

If the hay box is efficient your porridge will be ready for you in the morning. Stews should be cooked for an hour before being put in the box.

In theory, putting food in a thermos flask should work just as well. In practice, it doesn't, not for me, anyway, although the subsequent cooking time of stews is considerably reduced, which is often helpful on holiday.

Chicken on a spit

You have missed a lot if you have never crouched in the dusk by a camp fire and tended a chicken roasting on a spit. There may be no wild animals roaring in the nearby forest, but I daresay the emotions of those who gaze into the glowing embers are much the same as those of our ancestors in similar circumstances. There will be contentment mixed with anticipation that soon the second of our most basic needs will be met. And afterwards, when the crisp golden bird has been dismembered and devoured, there will be a drowsy feeling of security and satisfaction never to be forgotten.

Since we undoubtedly have primitive man to thank for our enjoyment, let's hope that he felt equally comfortable as he tossed another log on his dying fire.

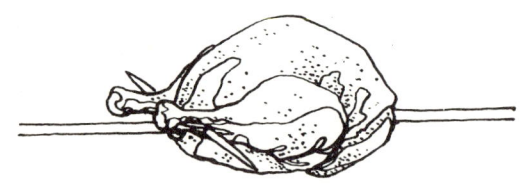

Potatoes in the embers To serve 4

you will need	8 medium-sized potatoes
	butter
	salt and pepper
equipment	*sharp knife*
	metal foil

You need good red embers for baking potatoes. Scrub them, prick them all over and wrap individually in foil. Put them in the embers, drawing the wood up round them. They should take about 45 minutes. Eat with lots of butter, salt and freshly ground black pepper. Or top them with grated cheese or bacon rolls.

They are good with kebabs, too. See pages 35 – 9.

Sausages in banana skins

you will need	sausages
	salt and pepper
equipment	*a banana skin for each*
	sausage
	fork

Remove the banana from its skin carefully, splitting it in one place only. Prick the sausage, season to taste and place in the banana skin, close the skin again neatly. Place in the embers for about 45 minutes.

The sausage will emerge perfectly cooked but not crisp. In fact, somewhat soggy. However, you may like to try it this way.

Apples in foil

you will need	4 or more large cooking apples soft brown sugar butter
equipment	*potato peeler* *knife* *teaspoon* *metal foil*

Wash the apples but do not peel. Core them, make a cut in the skin right round with the point of a knife, and fill the centre with brown sugar. Put a small piece of butter on each one and seal tightly in metal foil. Place in the embers of your fire, and if it is a good cooking fire the apples should take 30 – 45 minutes.

Twists

you will need	4 oz. self-raising flour 1 level teaspoon salt water
equipment	*mixing bowl* *blunt knife* *peeled green sticks* *some good red embers*

Mix the flour and salt with enough water to make a stiff dough. Then with floured hands twist a lump of the dough round the end of a thick peeled stick. Don't use a dry stick or your twist may end in the fire just when it is beautifully brown all round.

Stick one end of your stick in the ground and prop it over

a log so that the twist is over the heat, and turn from time to time.

Twists are the camper's traditional substitute for bread. They should be eaten hot with butter and jam or cheese.

Eggs in oranges

you will need	eggs
	salt and pepper
	butter
equipment	*one orange for each 2 eggs*
	knife and spoon
	metal foil

Remove the pulp from the orange by halving it and carefully scraping out the flesh. Butter each half, break in an egg, dust with salt and pepper and cover firmly with metal foil. Place in rather cool embers for about 20 minutes.

Baked cheese bread To serve 4

you will need	1 crusty French loaf
	4 oz. butter or garlic butter, see page 197
	4 oz. sharp Cheddar cheese, grated
equipment	*knife and chopping board*
	metal foil

Cut the loaf in half, lengthwise. Spread generously with the butter or garlic butter. Cover with grated cheese. Wrap loaf firmly in foil, sealing the edges well, and place in the embers or on a barbecue grill until butter runs into bread and cheese melts. Serve with tomato salad, see pages 69 and 70.

Baked potatoes with prawns and eggs

you will need
2 hard-boiled eggs
1 small can prawns
4 tablespoons oil
2 tablespoons vinegar
salt and pepper
8 medium-sized potatoes baked in embers,
see page 27

equipment
bowl
knife
can opener
tablespoon
jug

Chop the peeled hard-boiled eggs and mix thoroughly with the prawns. Combine oil and vinegar, add salt and pepper to taste, pour over egg and prawn mixture and mix well.

Open the foil in which each potato is wrapped and fold back. Make a deep slit in the top of each potato and press in the dressed egg and prawn mixture.

Fondue bourguignonne To serve 4

you will need
1½ lb. fillet steak
4 oz. butter
salt and pepper

equipment
good heavy frying pan
4 forks
4 large plates

Cut all the fat off the steak and chop it into 1-inch cubes. Give everyone a share of the butter and heat the frying

30

pan, well supported, over the fire. Now let them cook their steak as they like it, piece by piece.

Serve with Garlic butter see page 197, or Cucumber with lemons, see page 170, or simply a mixture of garlic and parsley, finely chopped.

With lots of crisp French bread, and butter, and a green salad, it's a feast.

Hamburgers on green sticks

To serve 4

you will need	1 egg
	1 lb. best quality mince
	½ small onion
	1 teaspoon marjoram
	salt and pepper
equipment	*bowl and fork*
	sharp knife and board
	teaspoon
	4 skewers or peeled
	green sticks

Beat the egg in the bowl and mix in the mince (canned mince is unfortunately not suitable), chopped onion, the marjoram, and salt and pepper to taste. Cook in egg-sized pieces squeezed firmly round the end of a stick.

Serve with red mustard sauce or Tabasco sauce, see pages 191 and 195.

Variations

Detach from the stick and serve in a split roll with: —
1. A slice of processed cheese spread with mustard or tomato ketchup.
2. Thin slices of tomato spread with bottled mayonnaise and sprinkled with chopped chives or finely chopped onion.

31

Kidneys in potatoes

you will need	8 medium-sized potatoes
	8 thin rashers streaky bacon
	4 lambs' kidneys
	salt and pepper
equipment	*knife*
	metal foil
	4 skewers or peeled
	green sticks

Wash the potatoes, prick all over and wrap in metal foil. Put into the hot embers for about 45 minutes.

Wrap strips of bacon around pieces of kidney and thread on to skewers, and put them over the fire when the potatoes have been cooking for about 30 minutes.

To serve, unwrap the potatoes, make a deep slit in the top of each, sprinkle with salt and pepper to taste and slide the kidneys and bacon into the slit.

Serve with green salad.

Garlic bread

you will need	4 oz. butter
	1 clove garlic
	salt and pepper
	1 crusty French loaf
equipment	*knife and chopping board*
	small bowl and fork
	metal foil

Cream the butter with the finely chopped garlic and salt and pepper to taste, and slice the loaf downwards, leaving about ½-inch still joined at the bottom. Spread the butter mixture between the slices.

Wrap the loaf firmly in foil, sealing the edges well, and place in the embers or on a barbecue grill until the butter runs into the bread and the loaf becomes even crustier.

Toasted sandwich

To serve 1

you will need	2 good rashers bacon
	2 slices bread
	1 tomato, sliced
	1 oz. cheese, sliced
	pepper
equipment	*knife*
	toothpicks
	forked stick
	frying pan

Fry the bacon until crisp. Now make a sandwich with all the ingredients and press the slices of bread firmly together. Secure with the toothpicks to stop the bread curling, and lay the sandwich on the forked stick to toast. Cook it slowly so that it heats right through and the cheese runs before the bread is browned.

Variations

1. Replace the fried bacon with cooked ham or boiled bacon.
2. Replace tomato with about 2 oz. mushrooms, lightly fried in the bacon fat.
3. Replace the tomato with thin slices of apple.
4. Use as a filling: a chopped soft-boiled egg, knob of butter, a little copped parsley, pinch of celery salt, seasoning to taste and thin slice of cheese.
5. Use as a filling: 2 oz. grated cheese, 1 tomato sliced, 2 teaspoons finely chopped celery.

Pork chops in foil

To serve 4

you will need	1 large cooking apple
	1 small onion
	4 good pork chops
	1 teaspoon sugar
	1 teaspoon marjoram
	salt and pepper
equipment	*knife and board*
	metal foil
	teaspoon

Chop the apple and the onion. Lay each chop on a piece of metal foil large enough to enclose it completely. Spread the apple, onion, sugar, marjoram and salt and pepper to taste, on each chop and wrap firmly in the foil.

Put into the hot embers. They should be cooked in about 30 minutes.

Sweet corn in foil

you will need	1 sweet corn cob per person
	softened butter
	salt
	freshly ground black pepper
equipment	*knife*
	metal foil

Remove husks and silk from the corn. Let stand in salted water for 20 minutes to 1 hour; then drain well. Brush corn with softened butter and sprinkle with salt and pepper. Wrap each cob securely in double thickness foil; twist ends well. Place in the embers or on a barbecue grill. Leave for about 10 minutes, turning once.

Kebabs

Kebabs are great fun to cook over an open fire or a barbecue grill. They are easy, and there are no saucepans to be washed afterwards. Incidentally, the easiest way to deal with dirty saucepans is to scour them with wet sand, one of the oldest of cleaning aids.

Kebabs can be as simple as you like or as sophisticated; from pork sausages browned all over and thrust into mustard spread rolls with a few onion rings, to beef kebabs in a Burgundy marinade.

By the time you are ready to start cooking, the fire should have quietened to some good red embers. The kebabs don't want to be smoked. Then with a good supply of stout peeled green sticks – they must be green or they will snap under the weight of the food – and the ingredients already cut up, you're in business. And by the way, if you see a backwoods type chewing the end of a green stick, it won't be because he can't wait for his meal, but to see if his improvised skewer has a bitter taste – some do.

Oil your skewer or stick, and if you are letting each member of the party cook his own kebabs it is a help if you pierce cubes of meat before handing them over, for easy threading.

Experiment will show the best way of arranging the sticks so that the food cooks evenly. One end of the stick can be pushed into the ground over a log so that the food-laden end is suspended over the fire. For a large party this works well. Another method is to build a small hunter's fire between two large logs, to thread the food on to the centre of the stick and to lay it across the fire with the ends resting on the logs. The latter method makes it easy to turn the kebabs.

Kebabs with bacon on them will baste themselves, but lean meat will need basting in oil or a marinading sauce from time to time. Take the sticks off the fire to baste the food to avoid flaring and smoke.

Kebabs can also be cooked over a charcoal grill.

Beef kebabs

you will need	1½ lb. fillet steak
	marinade, see recipe
	4 oz. mushrooms
	2 sweet green peppers
equipment	*knife and chopping board*
	4 skewers or green sticks,
	peeled

Cut the steak into 1-inch cubes and marinate for 2−3 hours in Burgundy marinade, see page 196. When you are ready to start cooking, drain the meat and thread steak on the skewers alternating with the mushroom caps and squares of green pepper. Cook over a wood fire or barbecue grill for about 5 minutes, or until the meat is cooked to your liking, basting from time to time with the marinading sauce.

Serve with boiled rice, see page 110.

Bacon, tomato and onion kebabs

you will need	1 lb. bacon
	8 small firm tomatoes
	2 onions
equipment	*knife and chopping board*
	4 long skewers or long
	peeled green sticks

Cut each rasher of bacon in 2 and roll. Score the skin of the tomatoes and peel and quarter the onions, removing the centre layers which are difficult to thread on skewers.

Load the skewers, alternating the bacon with the tomatoes and onions. Cook over the embers or on a barbecue grill, turning frequently until the bacon is crisp.

Serve with potato crisps heated on the fire in foil, or potatoes baked in their jackets. See page 27.

Spanish fried rice is also delicious with kebabs. Made with 8 oz. rice, 2 oz. margarine or olive oil, 1 onion and a pint of boiling water. You fry chopped onion until tender. Add rice and fry, shaking well. When rice has absorbed fat add boiling water. Season and simmer slowly for 20 minutes. The water will be absorbed and the rice will be tender and with each grain separate.

Kidney, bacon and sausage kebabs

To serve 4

you will need	8 oz. chipolata sausages
	8 oz. lambs' kidneys
	8 oz. bacon rashers
equipment	*knife*
	4 skewers or peeled
	green sticks

Divide each sausage in two by pressing gently with thumb and middle finger in the centre to separate the meat, then twisting and cutting in two. Prick all over. Cut the kidneys into pieces and wrap pieces of bacon loosely round each piece of kidney and each sausage. Thread alternately on the skewers and grill for about 20 minutes, not too close to the fire.

37

Pork and pineapple kebabs

To serve 4

you will need	1½ lb. fillet of pork 1 medium-sized can pineapple chunks ¼ pint olive oil salt and pepper
equipment	*sharp knife and board* *can opener* *measuring jug* *shallow bowl and spoon* *4 skewers or peeled sticks*

Cut the pork into 1-inch cubes and put in the bowl. Mix the juice from the canned pineapple with the oil and salt and pepper to taste and pour over the pork. Drain well and thread the pork alternately with the pineapple on the skewers. Grill over a wood fire or barbecue grill for about 25 minutes, basting frequently with the oil and pineapple juice.

Lamb kebabs

To serve 4

you will need	1½ lb. shoulder of lamb marinade, see recipe 2 onions 8 small mushrooms
equipment	*sharp knife and board* *4 skewers or peeled* *green sticks*

Cut the lamb into 1-inch cubes, removing most of the fat but leaving enough to baste the meat. Marinade overnight or as long as possible in Mint and onion sauce, see page 194, or Cider and lemon marinade, see page 196.

When you are ready to cook, quarter the onions, drain the meat, and remove the mushroom caps. Thread alternately on the skewers and cook over the hot embers, turning from time to time and basting frequently with the marinade, for about 20 minutes.

Other Kebabs

Practically any combination of meat and vegetable or fruit can be successfully turned into kebabs — the permutations are almost endless. Here are a few mixtures that my family like: —

Cooked pieces of chicken wrapped in bacon, alternated with mushroom caps and tomatoes. Good with Lemon barbecue sauce, see page 194.

Cubes of canned ham with quartered onions and apple segments. This one needs frequent basting with oil or a sauce with oil in it. See page 192.

Halved sausages and pineapple chunks. Canned sausages do very well.

Halved frankfurters with quartered apples. Good dunked in red mustard sauce. See page 191.

Pineapple chunks wrapped in bacon and served with fresh tomato salad and watercress.

Cubes of beef tossed in oil with mushroom caps. If you have more time than money use chuck steak braised in one piece and cubed for grilling.

Chicken pieces with squares of sweet green pepper and quartered onions, basted in butter.

Plump cooked prunes wrapped in bacon.

Cubes of ham with quartered bananas wrapped in bacon.

Pieces of liver with bacon and mushrooms.

Cooking on
a barbecue

On organised camp sites where open fires are taboo the portable barbecue is a near perfect substitute. Cooking over charcoal opens up new and interesting avenues of cooking.

When buying a charcoal-fired barbecue don't be tempted to buy a big one for camping purposes. Bags of charcoal—usually weighing 7 lb—are expensive compared with bottled gas and good old-fashioned paraffin. But barbecue cookery adds a special flavour all of its own.

The hibachi, a barbecue that originated in Japan, has proved to be very popular because of its simplicity and low cost. Round or rectangular hibachis are available in two styles, either table top or free-standing, and there are now lightweight versions made from pressed steel or aluminium instead of heavy cast black metal.

Picnic barbecues are also available in several styles. They are small, usually round in shape and are adequate for up to eight people. Some models have a wind shield and a few incorporate a spit.

Whatever type of barbecue you choose, make sure it is completely stable. Grills should be made of nickel and chrome-plated steel, with bars that are close enough to stop food falling through. Spits and spit forks should also be of heavy chrome-plated steel to prevent them bending with the weight of food.

No one can tell you just how to manage a charcoal fire. The knack is something which has to be learnt. But here are a few hints to start with.

Start to light the fire at least 45 minutes before you intend to start cooking. Remove the grill and make a heap of charcoal in the middle of the hearth about 6 inches across and as high as you can pile it. Place small pieces of fire-lighters amongst the charcoal—never use paraffin which will taint the food. Light the fire-lighters with a match or taper; when the flames have subsided some of the central coals will have caught alight and begun to glow. Waft the mound gently until the glow spreads. When the whole mound has begun to glow right through, ease it over towards the back of the hearth and cover with a fresh layer of charcoal. Leave to burn through nicely—when it looks white it is ready to cook over.

Now is the time to insert the grill, oil it lightly and pop on the food. A circular rotating grill is probably the easiest to manage as the food can be brought over the exact amount of heat needed, and can be brought to the front of the hearth where there is no fire for basting, which will save a lot of flaring and spluttering. An old squeezy lemon filled with water is ideal for dousing if the charcoal **should** flare.

Steaks and skewered food will need a hot fire, chops and sausages call for gentler heat. So will hamburgers and gammon steaks.

Baste non-fatty foods from time to time. Fish wrapped in foil with seasoning and a pat of butter cooks beautifully in the empty space in front of the hearth. Turn it after about 15 minutes. Vegetables can be cooked in this way, too, but all food that is wrapped in foil will be minus that unique charcoal taste which is so pleasant.

A pair of metal tongs is better for tending the food than a fork. Beware of making the portions so small that they fall through the grid. Never scour the grill with steel wool—little bits break off and stick to the food. Clean it instead with a stiff brush.

Sprigs of marjoram or a cut clove of garlic tossed on to the glowing coals about ten minutes before cooking is complete imparts a wonderful flavour to the meat. And you can throw in strips of orange peel when you are cooking gammon.

That's the thing about cooking on a barbecue grill. The more you do the more ideas come to mind.

Hamburgers

To serve 4

you will need	1 egg
	1 lb. good minced steak
	1 small onion, chopped
	salt and pepper
	1 tablespoon chopped parsley
	little flour
equipment	*mixing bowl and fork*

Beat the egg in the bowl, add the steak, onion, salt and pepper and parsley. Mix well. Shape into balls with floured hands, flatten and put on the barbecue grill. Turn when the underside is nicely browned. A clove of garlic thrown into the charcoal makes the hamburgers smell and taste delicious.

Serve with one of the Barbecue sauces, see pages 192—3.

Charcoal cooked halibut

To serve 4

you will need	4 halibut steaks
	2 oz. butter
	juice $\frac{1}{2}$ lemon
	salt and pepper
	chopped parsley
equipment	*metal foil*

Lay each steak on a piece of metal foil large enough to enclose in completely. Dot each steak with butter, squeeze the lemon juice over it, add salt and pepper to taste and sprinkle the chopped parsley on top. Make a parcel of each steak, closing the edges of the foil firmly. Put the parcels into the charcoal, which should be only moderately hot. The steaks should be cooked in 25—30 minutes.

Barbecued fillet
of pork

To serve 4

you will need	1½ lb. pork fillet
	1 eating apple
	juice of 1 lemon
	1 egg
	breadcrumbs
	olive oil
	chopped parsley
	4 tomatoes
	1 medium packet frozen peas
	boiled rice, see page 110
	salt and pepper
equipment	*chopping board*
	sharp knife
	small jug
	fork
	lemon squeezer
	plate
	small brush for
	basting
	saucepan for rice

Split the fillet lengthwise or ask the butcher to do it for you, and cut it into 4 portions. Peel and core the apple, cut it into 4 rings and dip in a little of the lemon juice to prevent discoloration.

Beat the egg with the rest of the lemon juice, dip the meat into this and then roll in the breadcrumbs so that the meat is evenly coated.

Paint with olive oil and grill over a moderate heat over charcoal, basting with oil from time to time. When golden brown underneath, turn.

Wrap the peas with seasoning and a knob of butter in metal foil, securing the edges firmly, and cook under the grill. Halve the tomatoes, season and paint them with oil, and grill.

Serve the pork on a bed of rice with peas and tomatoes, and an apple ring on each portion of meat.

Charcoal grilled langoustine

To serve 4

you will need	8 – 12 langoustine tails
	2 oz. butter
	salt
	freshly milled black pepper
	lemon
equipment	*sharp knife and board*
	lemon squeezer
	charcoal grill

Lay tails on back and slice in $\frac{1}{2}$ lengthwise. Paint exposed meat with a little melted butter. Place tail halves shell down on the grill and cook over moderate heat until the white meat turns faintly brown, basting with more butter from time to time. Season to taste and sprinkle with lemon juice before serving.

Serve with crisp French bread and butter, and a salad or Cold cucumber sauce, see page 188.

Variations

Any shellfish – sold in different countries as Dublin Bay prawns, crayfish, lobster tails, Norwegian lobsters, crawfish, scampi – of this type can be grilled in this way.

Basque grilled gammon

To serve 4

you will need	1 small can tomatoes
	2 sweet green peppers
	1 clove garlic
	1 tablespoon olive oil
	salt and pepper
	sugar
	4 good gammon rashers
	2 eggs
	French loaf
	butter
equipment	*small saucepan*
	can opener
	chopping board
	sharp knife
	tablespoon
	wooden spoon
	charcoal grill
	small basting brush
	for oil

Drain the canned tomatoes. De-seed the sweet pepper and slice it finely, chop the garlic and fry them both gently in the olive oil. Add the tomatoes, salt and pepper and a little sugar, stir well and leave over a cool part of the grill whilst you grill the gammon over a moderate heat, having first removed the rind and slashed the fat to prevent the slices from curling. Baste from time to time with its own fat.

When the gammon is nearly cooked, add the eggs to the tomato mixture and beat them in quickly. Cook for a few more minutes and pour over the gammon to serve.

Eat immediately with buttered French bread.

Barbecued chicken

To serve 4

you will need	1 2½ lb. chicken ¼ pint white wine 1 chopped onion 1 tablespoon olive oil squeeze lemon juice pinch tarragon salt and pepper
equipment	*saucepan and lid* *ladle*

Cut the chicken into serving pieces. Mix all the other ingredients thoroughly and leave the chicken pieces to marinade in the liquid for several hours. Stew gently for 45 minutes.

Drain the chicken pieces, grill over charcoal, basting with the liquid, until crisp and golden.

Cheese and eggs

Cheese and eggs are two of the most useful ingredients of the camp larder or food locker. They can both be used in many ways—there is enormous variety in omelettes alone. And in hot weather both travel more satisfactorily than fresh meat to provide necessary protein.

Cheese with rice and shrimps

To serve 4

you will need	8 oz. boiled rice, see page 110
	2 oz. butter
	2 teaspoons curry powder
	1 medium-sized can shrimps
	8 oz. Cheddar cheese
equipment	*frying pan*
	wooden spoon
	can opener
	grater or potato peeler

Drain the boiled rice well. Melt the butter and stir in the curry powder, then add the rice and mix well. Drain the canned shrimps and add to the pan, and stir in the grated cheese. Mix well and serve immediately the cheese starts to melt. Serve with lots of green salad.

Macaroni cheese

you will need	4 oz. grated cheese
	1 small can evaporated milk
	½ level teaspoon dry mustard
	salt and pepper
	6 oz. macaroni
	1 tomato
	little olive oil
	parsley
equipment	*large saucepan*
	fireproof serving dish or tin
	steamer and bowl to fit over
	* saucepan, or bowl with lugs*
	can opener
	knife
	teaspoon
	small brush

Put plenty of water to boil in the saucepan. Mix the grated cheese, milk, mustard, and salt and pepper to taste, in the bowl. When the water in the pan boils, pour a little into the heatproof dish to warm it, salt the remainder, add the macaroni and bring to the boil again. Cook the cheese mixture in the bowl over the macaroni until the sauce thickens and the macaroni is tender. Mind it doesn't boil over.

When the macaroni is cooked, drain it and combine with the sauce. Turn into the heated serving dish, garnish with the sliced tomato painted with oil and brown under the grill. Serve decorated with parsley sprigs.

Spanish tortilla

you will need	1 large potato
	1 small onion
	3 tablespoons olive oil
	3 eggs
	1 tablespoon water
	salt and pepper
equipment	*knife and board*
	frying pan
	spatula
	jug or bowl
	fork
	tablespoon

Peel and dice the potato and chop the onion. Heat the oil in the frying pan and brown the vegetables, stirring now and then.

Beat the eggs lightly with the water and salt and pepper to taste and pour into the pan with the onion and potato.

Let the eggs begin to set, tilting the pan and lifting the mixture so that the eggs will run underneath and cook.

When the bottom is set, turn the omelette over and cook the other side.

The surfaces should be golden but the inside should still be moist.

Very satisfying with fresh bread and butter and firm ripe tomatoes.

French omelette

you will need	3 eggs
	1 tablespoon water
	salt and pepper
	½ oz. butter
equipment	*bowl for mixing*
	fork
	tablespoon
	7-inch frying pan, preferably
	with rounded sides
	fish slice or spatula

Beat the eggs lightly with the water and salt and pepper. Heat the frying pan, put in the butter and immediately it has melted pour in the eggs. Leave for 10 seconds to let the eggs set a little, then stir with a fork once or twice. Spread any chosen filling on to the omelette, then tilt the pan and move the omelette slightly to one side so that any uncooked mixture will run back on to the bottom of the pan. Fold the omelette over and serve immediately on a hot plate.

Not everyone will agree, but I like to make omelettes in a small non-stick pan, which necessitates a spatula instead of a fork, for stirring.

Suggested fillings:

Chopped kidney and onion fried in butter
Peeled, chopped tomato
Mushrooms
Diced potato fried until golden before the egg is added
Omelette Provencale – chopped tomatoes, onion and garlic, fried in oil
Chopped bacon or chopped ham
1 oz. grated cheese
Shrimps or prawns
Thin strips of sweet pepper and diced luncheon meat
Diced cucumber and ham

Scrambled eggs

Scrambled eggs have one great advantage over omelettes for holiday cooking, namely that they can be cooked in bulk whereas omelettes should be made for one person at a time. All the suggested fillings for omelettes can be served with, or stirred into, scrambled eggs if you want to be sociable and all eat together.

To serve 4

you will need	8 eggs
	8 tablespoons milk
	salt and pepper
	2 oz. butter
equipment	*large pan*
	wooden spoon
	tablespoon

Again I like to use a non-stick pan because it makes the washing up so much less nasty. Despite advice from some authorities, I just put all the eggs, milk, salt and pepper and 1 oz. butter into a pan.

Then I stir it all up vigorously with the wooden spoon and put it on the heat and leave for about 30 seconds while I bully someone into making the toast. Then I stir the gorgeous mixture tenderly until it begins to set, being very careful never to let it boil, and as soon as it's almost done I stir in the other oz. of butter and dish it up straight away.

Note:

For lightweight campers, dried Omelet mix is sometimes useful. The flavour is good and the texture rather akin to that of Scrambled eggs. Any of the foregoing fillings can be used with the Omelet mix, and it is particularly successful used in a Basque omelette, see below, or an Omelette Provençale.

Basque omelette

you will need
2 tomatoes
1 sweet green pepper
1 onion
1 clove garlic
little olive oil or bacon fat
2 oz. chopped ham
salt and pepper
1 packet Omelet mix

equipment
sharp knife
frying pan
wooden spoon

Peel the tomatoes by dipping in hot water for a minute. Chop the vegetables and fry lightly with the ham and salt and pepper to taste. When they are soft, stir in the prepared Omelet mix and cook for a few minutes longer.

Halliwell's fry

To serve 4

you will need
2 oz. butter
1½ lb. cooked potatoes
salt and pepper
1 large onion
1 small packet frozen peas
8 oz. Cheddar cheese
2 peeled tomatoes

equipment
large frying pan and lid
knife and chopping board
fish slice

Heat the butter in the frying pan, add the sliced potatoes and fry until golden brown underneath. Season. Chop the

54

onion and add these to the pan with the peas. Cut the cheese into ½-inch cubes, put on top of the peas and onions and sprinkle with pepper. Top with sliced tomatoes and heat through gently until the cheese has melted.

Fondue

To serve 4

you will need	1 lb. grated Cheddar cheese
	¼ pint dry cider
	2 eggs
	salt and pepper
	¼ teaspoon Worcestershire sauce
equipment	*double saucepan or bowl to fit on to saucepan*
	wooden spoon

Melt the cheese in the top of the double saucepan and add the cider a little at a time, stirring. Then stir in the beaten eggs and season to taste. Add Worcestershire sauce.

Serve when thick with French bread or thick toast cut into cubes.

Cheese and potato cakes

To serve 4

you will need	8 oz. grated Cheddar cheese
	1 lb. freshly mashed potatoes
	4 oz. fine breadcrumbs
	2 oz. stoned raisins, chopped
	1 egg
equipment	*large bowl*
	frying pan

Put cheese, potatoes, breadcrumbs and raisins into bowl. Mix well and season. Add beaten egg to make soft dough.

Form into cakes and fry in hot bacon fat until golden brown.
Serve with apple sauce.

Gloucestershire cheese mash

To serve 4

you will need	3½-oz. packet instant potato
	¾ pint water
	3 tablespoons milk
	1 oz. butter
	2 oz. flour
	4 oz. grated cheese
	chopped parsley
	salt
	freshly ground black pepper
	fat for frying
equipment	*large saucepan*
	tablespoon
	cup
	fork
	large frying pan
	fish slice or spatula

Prepare the instant potato according to the directions on
the packet.

Add the flour and the cheese and beat. Whisk the egg
and work it into the mixture together with the chopped
parsley and seasonings.

Melt the fat in the frying pan, add the cheese and potato
mixture and smooth down.

Brown the underside over a moderate heat, divide into
4 portions with the spatula and turn so that both sides are
browned.

Serve with cold meat and a tomato salad.

Eggs Mornay

you will need	Mornay sauce, see page 186
	8 fresh eggs
	3½ oz. packet instant potato
	milk
	butter
	salt and pepper
	additional grated cheese
equipment	*saucepan for sauce*
	large shallow pan for poaching
	saucepan and lid for potato
	fork
	perforated spoon
	grater or potato peeler
	heatproof serving dish

Prepare the Mornay sauce, using ½ pint milk and 3 oz. grated cheese, and put a lid over the pan.

Poach the eggs gently, and while they are cooking prepare the mashed potato according to the instructions on the packet.

Turn the mashed potato into the serving dish and make 8 depressions with the back of a spoon for the eggs. Drain the eggs well as soon as they are cooked, pour the Mornay sauce on to them and top with a little additional grated cheese.

Brown quickly under the grill or salamander.

Salads

On a blistering summer's day what could be more perfect than a bowlful of cool colourful salad?

Choose your ingredients for colour contrast and different textures as well as flavour, and dress them simply with olive oil and lemon or vinegar, salt and pepper and perhaps a few herbs. Turn them thoroughly to ensure that everything is well coated with dressing and shining attractively.

If you've pitched your tent in some corner of a foreign field it's a good idea to add a few drops of Milton to the water when you wash your salad stuffs. It won't taste, and it MAY save the more susceptible members of the party from discomfort.

Coleslaw

To serve 4

you will need	1 small white hard cabbage
	½ small onion
	1 oz. chopped almonds
	2 eating apples
	1 teaspoon sugar
	Quick salad dressing, see page 190
equipment	*knife and board*
	salad bowl
	teaspoon

Remove the stump and thick ribs from the cabbage and shred it very finely. Chop the onion, almonds and apple very finely and mix with the cabbage. Sprinkle with the sugar and add enough Quick salad dressing to coat all the ingredients.

Tuna and orange salad To serve 4

you will need
   2 heads chicory
   2 good oranges
   2 6½-oz. cans tuna
   2 clusters black grapes
   2 hard-boiled eggs

equipment
   large platter or
     metal foil
   jug
   sharp knife and board
   can opener

Remove any discoloured leaves from the chicory, wash it and shake dry. Arrange it round the edge of the platter, or spread foil on a tray. Pour boiling water over the oranges, leave to stand for 2 minutes, then peel. Slice and lay on the chicory. Break the tuna into chunks and place in the centre of the platter with the grapes at each end. Slice the eggs and put on top of the orange.

Serve with cold cucumber sauce, see page 188 and wholemeal bread and butter.

Canadian salad To serve 4

you will need
   3 oranges
   6 firm tomatoes
   2 dessertspoons tomato ketchup

equipment
   small jug or bowl
   knife and board
   lemon squeezer
   serving dish

Put 2 of the oranges into the jug and pour boiling water over them. Leave for 1 minute to loosen the peel. Slice the tomatoes, peel the oranges, slice, and add to the tomatoes. Squeeze the third orange, mix the juice with the tomato ketchup and pour over the oranges and tomatoes.

An unusual combination of flavours, good with pork.

Summer fish salad

you will need	4 whiting
	1 tablespoon olive oil
	1 tablespoon lemon juice
	¼ teaspoon paprika
	¾ teaspoon mixed herbs
	1 lettuce
	4 firm tomatoes
	½ cucumber
equipment	*frying pan and lid*
	tablespoon
	teaspoon
	fish slice
	sharp knife
	serving dish

Ask the fishmonger to fillet the fish for you or do it yourself. Poach very gently in the covered frying pan in a liquid made from the oil, lemon juice, paprika and herbs.

The fish should be tender in about 15 minutes. Leave to get cold.

Arrange the washed and shaken lettuce on the serving dish, lay the fish on top and pour the liquid from the pan over it.

Garnish with slices of tomato and cucumber.

Tossed cheese and orange salad

To serve **4**

you will need	1 lettuce
	2 oranges
	8 oz. Cheddar cheese
	4 oz. cashew nuts
	1 tablespoon olive oil
	1 tablespoon lemon juice
	salt and pepper
equipment	*salad bowl*
	knife
	tablespoon

Wash and dry the lettuce. Tear coarsely and put into the bowl, then add the peeled oranges divided into segments. Cut the cheese into cubes and add to the bowl with the nuts. Dress with olive oil, lemon juice, season to taste.

Beetroot in French dressing

To serve **4**

you will need	1 lb. cooked beetroot
	2 sticks celery
	1 onion
	2 springs parsley
	1 clove garlic
equipment	*knife and board*
	salad bowl

Slice the beetroot and chop all the other ingredients finely. Mix all together in the bowl and dress with French dressing, see page 189. Alternatively Vinaigrette dressing may be used.

Cauliflower in French dressing

To serve 4

you will need	1 good cauliflower
	salt
	1 teaspoon lemon juice
	French dressing, see page 189
equipment	*knife*
	lemon squeezer
	saucepan and lid
	serving dish

Remove the outer leaves from the cauliflower and trim the stem and divide into flowerets. Cook in boiling, salted water, to which you have added the lemon juice, for about 10 minutes. The flowerets should be tender but still whole.

Put them into the serving dish when you have drained them, and when they are cold pour the French dressing over them, ensuring that each floweret is coated with the dressing.

Potato salad

To serve 4

you will need	1½ lb. cooked potatoes
	1 small onion
	2 tablespoons chopped parsley
	French dressing, see page 189
equipment	*knife and chopping board*
	tablespoon
	salad bowl

Boil the potatoes without peeling and remove the skins while they are still warm. Cool, and dice. Chop onion finely, mix with the potato and parsley, and turn in the dressing.

Chicory and orange salad

you will need	3 good heads of chicory
	2 oranges
	French dressing, see page 189
equipment	*knife and board*
	small bowl or jug
	salad bowl

Wash the chicory and dry well, then chop into ½-inch pieces. Pour boiling water on the oranges, leave for 1 minute, then peel them, chop coarsely and mix with the chicory in the salad bowl. Coat with French dressing, mix well, and serve immediately.

Prawn and avocado salad

To serve 4

you will need	2 ripe avocado pears
	lemon juice
	6 oz. prawns, fresh or canned
	vinaigrette dressing, see page 190
	paprika pepper
equipment	*knife*
	lemon squeezer
	can opener
	small bowl

The first time that I tried avocado pears I decided that I didn't like them. It wasn't until years afterwards that I found that I had tasted unripe ones, and that really they were quite delightful. The difference in flavour is quite remarkable.

Test them by pressing the stem ends gently. They should be slightly soft.

Cut the pears in half, lengthways, remove the stones and coat with lemon juice. Mix together the prawns and vinaigrette dressing, pile on to the pears and dust with the paprika.

Stuffed egg salad

To serve 4

you will need	6 hard-boiled eggs
	3 oz. butter
	4-oz. can tuna
	4 oz. cottage cheese
	¼ pint Béchamel sauce, see page 185
	salt and pepper
	6 oz. long-grain rice
	½ sweet red pepper
	4½-oz. packet frozen peas, cooked
	½ cucumber or diced cooked carrot
	French dressing, see page 189
	1 bunch watercress
	8 oz. tomatoes
equipment	*2 small bowls*
	fork
	saucepan for rice
	can opener
	knife and chopping board
	large serving dish

Peel the eggs and cut in half lengthways. Mash 3 yolks in each bowl with half the butter. Add tuna fish to one bowl and cheese to the other and enough Béchamel sauce to give a smooth mixture. Season to taste.

Cook the rice, see page 110, and mix with the de-seeded, chopped pepper, the peas and the cucumber or carrot. Moisten with the French dressing and adjust the seasoning.

Arrange the rice salad on the serving dish, place the egg whites on top and fill with the cheese and fish mixtures alternately. Garnish with watercress and sliced tomatoes.

Royal slaw

you will need	1 small red cabbage
	2 sticks celery
	1 apple
	1 banana
	French dressing, see page 189 or
	cheese dressing, see page 191
equipment	*knife and chopping board*
	salad bowl

Shred the cabbage finely, removing the stalk, chop the celery, apple and banana and mix together in the salad bowl. Dress with the chosen dressing.

Basque sardines

you will need	4 tomatoes
	2 onions
	1 sweet green pepper
	2 cans large sardines
	salt and pepper
	2 hard-boiled eggs
equipment	*jug or bowl*
	knife and board
	frying pan and lid
	can opener
	fish slice

Make a cross in the top of each tomato with a sharp knife, put them in the jug and pour boiling water over them to loosen the skins.

Fry the chopped onion and the sliced, de-seeded sweet pepper in the oil from the sardine cans, and when they are soft add the peeled and sliced tomatoes, season to taste, and cook for a few minutes more.

Now add the sardines and return to the heat until the fish are warmed through.

Dish the mixture up very carefully and garnish with sliced hard-boiled egg.

Serve with crisp French bread and Normandy butter.

American pineapple and cherry salad

To serve 4

you will need	1 packet black currant jelly
	1 small can cherries
	1 medium-sized can pineapple pieces
	8 oz. cottage cheese
	2 tablespoons cream
equipment	*heatproof measuring jug*
	can opener
	wooden spoon
	serving dish
	tablespoon
	small bowl

Put the jelly into the measuring jug and just cover with very hot water. Stir until dissolved. Remove the stones from the cherries and add them, with their juice, to the jelly. Drain the pineapple pieces and add enough of their juice to the jelly to make up to 1 pint, or a little less in very hot weather. Pour into the serving dish and leave to set.

When set, mix together the pineapple pieces, cottage cheese and cream, and spread over the jelly.

Serve with cold meat.

Sydney shrimp bouchées

To serve 4

you will need	4 tablespoons tomato chutney
	4 oz. sultanas
	1 small can prawns
	8 vol-au-vent cases
equipment	*small saucepan*
	teaspoon
	knife

Heat the chutney, sultanas and prawns in the saucepan. When really hot fill the vol-au-vent cases with the mixture and serve immediately.

Thursday patties

To serve 4

you will need	1 lb. sausage meat
	1 lettuce
	1 large can pineapple rings
	4 firm tomatoes
	1 oz. dripping
equipment	*frying pan and lid*
	fish slice
	serving dish
	sharp knife

Form the sausage meat into 12 flat rounds and fry on both sides until golden brown. Allow to become quite cold. Meanwhile, wash and drain the lettuce and arrange on the serving dish. Set out the patties, top each one with a ring of pineapple and then a slice of tomato.

Serve with plenty of fresh soft rolls and butter.

Tomato salad 1

you will need	6 firm ripe tomatoes
	1 teaspoon sugar
	salt and pepper
	juice 1 lemon
	chopped mint
equipment	*knife and chopping board*
	serving dish
	teaspoon
	lemon squeezer

Slice the tomatoes thinly, add the sugar and salt and pepper to taste, dress with the lemon juice and sprinkle with the chopped mint.

Delightfully flavoursome and cool on a hot day.

Sweet pepper salad

you will need	2 or 3 sweet green or red peppers
	lettuce
	French dressing,
	see page 189
equipment	*forks or peeled*
	green sticks
	knife and board
	serving dish

Grill the peppers or impale them on sticks and hold over an open fire until the skins are charred all over. Rub the skins off under water. Take out the seeds and slice finely.

Serve in French dressing on a bed of lettuce leaves.

Courgettes salad

To serve 4

you will need	1 lb. courgettes
	1 tablespoon olive oil
	salt and pepper
	1 teaspoon mixed herbs
	vinaigrette dressing, see page 190
equipment	*knife*
	tablespoon
	teaspoon
	frying pan
	salad bowl

Blanch the courgettes in boiling water for 2 or 3 minutes. Drain, cut in slices and fry gently in the olive oil until tender. Allow to cool, season to taste add herbs and dress with the vinaigrette dressing.

Tomato salad 2

To serve 4

you will need	1 lb. tomatoes
	3 dessertspoons olive oil
	1 dessertspoon wine vinegar
	salt
	black pepper
	1 teaspoon chopped parsley
equipment	*shallow bowl*
	chopping board and knife

Slice the tomatoes and place them in a shallow serving bowl. Mix the oil and vinegar with salt and black pepper. Pour this sauce over the tomatoes, sprinkle with parsley and serve. A little chopped onion or green pepper very finely chopped can replace the parsley in this dish.

Golden potato salad

To serve 6

you will need	1½ lb. cold boiled potatoes
	1 small onion, chopped
	2 tablespoons chopped parsley
	4 tablespoons chopped celery
	1 teaspoon salt
	2 tablespoons single cream
	2 tablespoons prepared mustard
	2 tablespoons sugar
	2 tablespoons vinegar
	¼ teaspoon salt
	good dash pepper
	crisp lettuce
equipment	*large bowl*
	chopping board and knife

In a large bowl, put diced potatoes, onion, parsley, celery and the 1 teaspoon salt and toss lightly. Combine cream and next five ingredients and beat until light and fluffy. Pour over the potato mixture and stir gently until well mixed. Let stand about 1 hour. Line a salad bowl with crisp lettuce and arrange potato salad on the top.

Fish

I suppose everyone's private escapist dreams include tugs at the rod, little wood fires, foaming butter at the ready and licking fishy fingers – from water to mouth in five minutes flat.

Except for the lucky few, it is likely to remain a dream. But we can help it along a bit on holiday, when we have time to buy our fish fresh from the beach, or at least from the fishmonger on the quay.

To those who live inland, the difference in flavour is nothing short of startling. And don't be put off by the fact that the fish you see landed may look unfamiliar – ask local people how THEY cook them.

If you are lucky you may be able to buy a bass – sometimes called bar or sea wold. In some places this noble fish is scorned, and sport fishermen who land it will be pleased to sell it to you, see page 82. Don't forget that there is a lot of waste with bass.

Here, for what it is worth, is a method of cooking freshwater fish which is reckoned in the Fens to do away with that peculiar muddy taste. I haven't tried it, you may like to.

You mustn't wash the fish. In fact you must disturb it as little as possible, because once the fish is limp and the special overlapping scales are disturbed the mud gets under them and touches the skin, which is absorbent.

Take hold of the head and working towards the tail encase it all in clay or a thick flour and water paste. Then grill it on a grid, slowly, first getting your grill pan very hot indeed because you won't be able to turn the fish without breaking the paste. On an open fire you can cook it on sticks laid across 2 logs, with the hot embers in between. Again you must cook it right through without turning it.

When it is thoroughly cooked, let it cool a little, and then you can break off the dry crust and the skin and scales will come away too. This is supposed to leave the fish with a beautiful clean flavour.

It sounds logical, but I can't vouch for it.

Fish in Mornay sauce To serve 4

you will need	1¼ lb. fillet of cod or haddock Mornay sauce, see page 186 3½ oz. packet instant potato milk butter salt and pepper
equipment	*shallow pan and lid* *heatproof serving dish* *saucepan and lid*

Poach the skinned fillets in just enough water to cover until tender. Drain well. In the meantime warm your serving dish and prepare the Mornay sauce, and just before the fish is cooked prepare the mashed potato according to the directions on the packet. Turn the mashed potato into the serving dish to form an attractive border. Flake the fish and add it to the Mornay sauce, and pour the fish and cheese mixture into the centre of the potato border.

Sprinkle with additional grated cheese and brown quickly under the grill, if liked.

Grilled cod steaks To serve 4

you will need	4 1-inch thick cod steaks 2 oz. butter salt and pepper little flour
equipment	*grill pan* *wooden spoon* *fish slice*

Remove the grid from the grill pan and melt the butter under a hot grill. Put in the steaks and turn them so that both sides are coated with butter. Sprinkle salt and pepper to taste, and a little flour, over the steaks. Baste them with the butter and grill until the bone can be easily removed. Adding a tablespoon of water to the pan will prevent drying out, and the steaks will need basting occasionally, but they will not need to be turned during cooking.

Serve with Mornay sauce or Tomato sauce, see page 186.

Portuguese cod
To serve 4

you will need	1 small onion
	2 oz. butter
	1 oz. flour
	1 medium-sized can tomatoes
	1 tablespoon wine vinegar
	salt and pepper
	2 tablespoons chopper parsley
	1½ lb. cod fillet
equipment	*large frying pan and lid*
	knife and chopping board
	can opener
	tablespoon
	wooden spoon
	fish slice
	asbestos mat

Fry the chopped onion gently in the butter until soft. Stir in the flour, then add the tomatoes and the vinegar and bring to the boil, stirring all the time. Add salt and pepper to taste and 1 tablespoon chopped parsley and simmer gently for 10 minutes. Divide the skinned fish into 4 pieces and add to the pan, spooning the tomato mixture over the fish so that it is completely covered. Bring to the boil again, then simmer very gently for about 10 minutes or until the fish is cooked and white.

Serve garnished with the remaining parsley.

Finnan haddock with poached eggs

To serve 4

you will need	1¼ – 1½ lb. finnan haddock 1 teaspoon salt 1 tablespoon vinegar 4 fresh eggs grated cheese
equipment	*large shallow pan with lid* *teaspoon* *tablespoon* *draining spoon*

Poach the haddock very gently in enough water to cover until tender. Remove from the water and keep warm. Skim off any scum, add salt and vinegar to the water and poach the eggs until just firm.

Serve an egg on each portion of haddock and sprinkle with grated cheese.

Grilled fresh haddock

To serve 4

you will need	1 clove garlic 1 tablespoon oil 2 oz. butter 1½ lb. fresh haddock fillets salt and pepper level tablespoon flour
equipment	*knife* *grill pan* *tablespoon*

Rub the cut clove of garlic all over the grill pan, then put in the oil and butter and heat but do not allow to burn.

Lay the skinned haddock in the pan and baste with the oil and butter. Season to taste and add a little water to the pan. Sprinkle the flour over the fillets.

Cook under the grill until rich golden brown, basting from time to time. Do not overcook and dry up the fish — if the grill pan is really hot before you start, 8 minutes should be enough and the fish will not need turning.

Serve with tomatoes — the canned round ones if you can find them — and lemon wedges.

Norwegian finnan haddock

To serve 4

you will need	1½ lb. smoked haddock
	8 oz. carrots
	2 oz. butter
	2 hard-boiled eggs
	salt and pepper
	parsley
equipment	*shallow pan and lid*
	asbestos mat
	knife and chopping board
	saucepan and lid
	draining spoon

Poach the haddock gently in enough water to cover for 10 minutes. Cook the peeled and sliced carrots in boiling salted water until tender. Drain both the haddock and the carrots, add the butter and chopped hard-boiled eggs to the carrots, mix gently and season to taste.

Serve the haddock divided into 4 pieces and topped with the carrot mixture. Garnish with plenty of chopped parsley.

Good with buttered soft rolls — and surprisingly filling.

Fried herrings

To serve 4

you will need   8 or more plump herrings
salt and pepper
medium oatmeal
olive oil

equipment   *sharp knife and board*
frying pan
fish slice

Fillet the herrings or ask the fishmonger to do it for you.
Roll them in the seasoned oatmeal and fry on both sides in
very hot oil.

In early summer you will need very little oil since the
herrings themselves will be very oily, but later in the year
you will need rather more.

Garnish with lemon wedges and sprigs of parsley.

Halibut with cucumber

To serve 4

you will need   2 oz. butter
1½ lb. halibut steak
salt and pepper
1 medium-sized can round tomatoes
1 teaspoon sugar
½ large cucumber

equipment   *frying pan and lid*
can opener
teaspoon
knife or potato peeler
dish and plate
weight

Melt the butter in the frying pan, put in the halibut and
season to taste. Cover the pan and fry very gently for about

20 minutes, or until the centre bone will come away easily. Baste occasionally.

When the fish is tender heap the tomatoes on top and sprinkle with the sugar. Heat through.

Meanwhile, cut the cucumber in paper thin slices, sprinkle with the salt, put in the dish and weight down. Pour off the liquid when ready to use, and arrange on top of the tomatoes. Serve immediately.

Marinated trout

To serve 4

you will need	8 small trout
	water
	vinegar
	1 teaspoon salt
	few peppercorns
	1 bay leaf
	sprig parsley
	1 small onion
	1 lemon
equipment	*knife and board*
	saucepan and lid
	teaspoon

Clean the trout and remove the heads and fins. Put into the saucepan with enough water and vinegar to cover, in the proportion ¼ vinegar to ¼ water.

Add the salt, peppercorns, bay leaf, parsley and sliced onion.

Bring to the boil, lower the heat and poach gently until tender.

Do not overcook. Let the fish become quite cold in the liquid in which it was cooked, then drain and serve.

Garnish with thin slices of lemon.

Mackerel with leeks and tomatoes

To serve 4

you will need	4 mackerel, filleted
	3 oz. butter
	1 small shallot, chopped
	2 leeks
	4 tomatoes
	salt and pepper
	juice $\frac{1}{2}$ lemon
equipment	*frying pan and lid*
	saucepan and lid
	knife and chopping board
	small jug
	lemon squeezer
	fish slice
	tablespoon

Sprinkle the mackerel with salt. Melt 2 oz. of butter in the frying pan and cook the mackerel gently with the lid on until tender.

Meanwhile, fry the shallot in the other 1 oz. of butter, and when soft add the white part of the leeks, cut in $\frac{1}{2}$-inch rounds.

Cook for 2−3 minutes. Pour boiling water over the tomatoes, skin them and remove the seeds, then chop them and add to the leeks and shallot.

Cover the pan and cook for about 15 minutes, or until the leeks are tender.

To serve, garnish the mackerel with the leek and tomato mixture and sprinkle with lemon juice.

Excellent with minted new potatoes.

Sprats with lemon

you will need	12 oz. fresh sprats 2 oz. flour 3 tablespoons olive oil 1 lemon parsley
equipment	*plate* *knife and board* *large frying pan* *fish slice*

Roll the cleaned sprats in flour and fry them in the oil over quite a fierce heat. Turn them when they are nicely browned on one side. Dish them up and garnish with lemon slices and parsley.

The sprats need to be eaten the moment they are cooked, so for 4 people you will need 2 sittings or 2 frying pans.

Kippers

To serve 4

you will need	4 pairs of kippers or more according to appetite
equipment	*large saucepan and well fitting lid*

Two thirds fill the saucepan with water and bring to the boil. Put in the kippers, cover tightly and remove from the heat. After the kippers have been in the water for 5 minutes they will be ready to eat.

Kipper lovers who live in bedsitters swear by this method, and it's certainly the most considerate for a camp site where you have neighbours; there is no smell.

I don't think the flavour compares with that of grilled or fried kippers.

Whiting with courgettes

To serve 4

you will need	4 good-sized whiting
	flour
	salt and pepper
	2 oz. butter
	1 lb. courgettes
	olive oil
	juice ½ lemon
	chopped parsley
equipment	*plate*
	2 frying pans
	knife and chopping board
	lemon squeezer

Ask the fishmonger to fillet the whiting for you. Coat it with flour, season to taste and fry in the butter. In the meantime, peel and dice the courgettes and fry in the oil.

To serve, spread the diced courgettes over the whiting, and sprinkle with the lemon juice and chopped parsley.

Bass with mushrooms To serve 4

you will need	12½ lb. sea bass
	4 oz. mushrooms
	2 tomatoes
	2 oz. butter
	salt and pepper
	juice 1 lemon
equipment	*knife and chopping board*
	large frying pan and lid
	lemon squeezer

Ask the fishmonger to bone the bass for you. Even if you

buy your bass from a fisherman on the beach, he will probably still do it for you.

Wash the fish and dry it. Fry the chopped mushrooms and the peeled and chopped tomatoes in the butter until soft, remove from the pan and stuff the fish. Season. Cook very gently in the remaining butter and the lemon juice in the covered pan until tender — about 30 minutes.

Cod braised with vegetables

To serve 4

you will need	1½ lb. cod fillet
	salt
	2 onions
	2 carrots
	2 sticks celery
	1 lb. potatoes
	4 tablespoons oil
	¼ pint water
	freshly ground black pepper
	juice of 1 large lemon
	chopped parsley
equipment	*chopping board*
	sharp knife
	colander or strainer
	large frying pan with lid
	lemon squeezer
	fish slice

Wash the fish and cut into 4 portions. Sprinkle with salt and leave to drain in a strainer or colander. Chop all the vegetables and put into the frying pan with the oil and water. Season to taste, cover the pan and simmer for about 15 minutes. Place the drained fish on top of the vegetables, pour the lemon juice over and simmer for a further 20 minutes over a very gently heat or until the fish is tender.

Sprinkle with chopped parsley before serving.

Sole in tomato sauce To serve 4

you will need	4 good fillets of sole
	juice ½ lemon
	flour
	salt and pepper
	olive oil
	6 tablespoons white wine
	2 tablespoons wine vinegar
	2 tablespoons tomato purée
	½ teaspoon sugar
	pinch crushed rosemary
	chopped parsley
equipment	*large frying pan*
	lemon squeezer
	plate
	fish slice
	tablespoon
	wooden spoon
	teaspoon
	knife and chopping board

Wash the fillets, sprinkle with lemon juice and dip in seasoned flour. Fry quickly in olive oil and remove from the pan. Add a little more oil to the pan and stir in 2 tablespoons of flour.

Cook for 2 minutes, stirring all the time.

Add all the rest of the ingredients except the parsley, stirring constantly until the sauce is thick and smooth, then add 3 tablespoons of water and bring to the boil again, still stirring. Simmer gently for about 15 minutes, then return the fish to the pan so that it becomes well coated with the sauce and thoroughly heated through.

Sprinkle with parsley before serving.

Plaice with orange sauce

To serve **4**

you will need	1 oz. butter
	1 onion
	2 large oranges
	1 tablespoon oil
	4 large fillets plaice
	1 oz. butter
	salt and pepper
	1 teaspoon cider vinegar
	1 teaspoon marjoram
equipment	*small saucepan*
	knife and chopping board
	lemon squeezer
	grater
	wooden spoon
	grill pan
	tablespoon
	teaspoon

Melt 1 oz. butter in the small pan and cook the finely chopped onion very gently until soft. Add the juice of 1 orange and the grated rind. Bring to the boil and take off the heat.

Oil the grill pan and heat. Lay the fillets in, dot with butter and season to taste. Grill.

Bring the orange sauce to the boil again, add the cider vinegar and marjoram, pour over the fish and garnish with the other orange cut into thin wedges.

Variation

Season grilled fillets, then cover each with several well drained asparagus heads. Cover with grated cheese and a little melted butter, and brown under the grill.

Fisherman's luck

To serve 4

you will need	4 oz. chopped green pepper
	4 oz. chopped onion
	2 tablespoons butter or margarine
	4 tablespoons tomato ketchup
	½ level teaspoon garlic salt
	2 small bay leaves
	4 halibut steaks (1-inch thick)
	salt and pepper
equipment	*chopping board and knife*
	frying pan
	metal foil

Cook the green pepper and onion in butter until they are tender but not brown. Add the ketchup, garlic salt, and the bay leaves. Simmer 10–15 minutes.

For each serving, cut a 28-inch length of metal foil and fold it in half.

Place 1 halibut steak in folded foil, just off centre; sprinkle with salt and pepper. Pour ¼ of the sauce over each serving of fish. Bring the foil up over the fish and sauce, so that edges meet on three open sides. Fold open edges towards food 2 or 3 times, in ½ inch folds. Press hard on all sides for a snug package. Cook over a glowing fire, turning once or twice, for 15–20 minutes.

Either snip off the folded ends of foil and transfer fish and sauce to a plate, or, cut a cross in the top of the package, fold the foil back and fish can be eaten from the package.

Skate with brown butter

you will need	4 pieces skate
	2 teaspoons capers
	seasoning
	3 oz. butter
	2 teaspoons chopped parsley
	2 teaspoons lemon juice or vinegar
equipment	*frying pan*
	saucepan

Put the skate into boiling salted water and cook gently for about 5 minutes. Lift out of water and pat dry. Heat the butter, put in the skate and fry steadily for about 10 minutes. Lift out on to a hot dish, then continue cooking butter until golden brown, adding the rest of the ingredients and seasoning well. Pour over the fish.

La bouillabaisse

Lovers of bouillabaisse, Larousse tells us, invest its preparation with divine origins. It seems that it was Vulcan's favourite dish, and in her heyday Venus fed it to him as a treat. This pleased both of them since it made him sleep particularly soundly and enabled Venus, like the whiting, to pursue her own ends.

Personally it's a dish I haven't eaten since I read Stephen Lister's book 'More Fit for a Bishop' and allowed myself to be persuaded that commercially made bouillabaisse is likely to be made from those marine creatures which lurk in the green slime of neglected corners of aquariums.

However, you may still like it, and if you find yourself near Marseilles you may even want to make it. One thing is certain, and that is that for a start you are going to need 8 or 10 people who can bring themselves to eat it when you've wrestled with it.

Here is the Larousse recipe for authentic Marseilles bouillabaisse, exquisite and succulent (sic).

La bouillabaisse

To serve 8 – 10

you will need	6½ lb. assorted fish from the following: — rascasse, chapon, saint-pierre, conger-eel, lophius, red mullet, rouquiet, whiting, sea-perch, spiny lobster, crabs, and other shellfish 2 large onions 8 cloves garlic 3 large tomatoes fennel, parsley bay leaf, thyme dry orange peel salt and pepper ¼ pint olive oil powdered saffron bread chopped parsley
equipment	*chopping knife and board* *enormous billycan or cauldron*

Cut all the fish into pieces of uniform size. Into the cauldron put the chopped onion and garlic, the peeled and chopped tomatoes, the herbs and the crumbled orange peel. Then add the crustacea, and on top the firm-fleshed fish. Season to taste, sprinkle with the olive oil and a good pinch of saffron, then add enough water to cover the fish. Boil briskly for 7 – 8 minutes, add the delicate-fleshed fish and continue to boil for another 6 – 7 minutes. Bouillabaisse must cook quickly.

Pour it all over home made bread to serve, and sprinkle with chopped parsley.

Meat

Traditional English cookery, calling for the very finest ingredients simply cooked, is frequently unsuitable for holiday trips.

You MAY, of course, find yourself with time to shop at leisure, guided by the advice of an old-fashioned family grocer or butcher. But you are equally likely to find yourself frantically filling a string bag with the nearest thing that comes to hand, mentally converting kilos to pounds, while the rest of the family disappear over the horizon shouting over their shoulders, Do come ON. We'll miss the TIDE.

There are some traditional English recipes in this section, like Sea pie, see page 149, which incidentally can be made very successfully from canned meat, but there are also peasant dishes from many parts which are particularly suitable for meals produced on fairly primitive cooking equipment.

The recipes for main dishes using cans are at the end of this section. There are times when cans are very, very useful. When we are far from the beaten track I'd rather open a can or two than wonder if the fresh meat we bought the day before is really safe to use despite that rather odd smell.

Canned meat can be used most successfully in fairly highly flavoured dishes such as curry, or in meat sauce for spaghetti. Frankfurters and ham can be used in a variety of dishes, or can be turned into delicious kebabs with mushrooms, onions, sweet green peppers, and so on.

If you prefer to serve your canned meat quite simply with vegetables, the meal will be wonderfully improved by the addition of a sauce. See page 184 onwards.

Fish also cans well, and can be the basis of many substantial meals. And as a not-too-tactful friend of mine once said to his hostess: 'What I always say is—prawns redeem anything!'

Pan fried steak

you will need	1½ lb. fillet or rump steak
	salt and pepper
	2 tablespoons oil
equipment	*rolling pin and board*
	frying pan
	tablespoon
	serving slice

Batter the steak with the rolling pin to flatten it and break down the fibres. Season. Heat the oil in the pan over a fierce heat, and when it is really hot fry the steak for about 1 minute on each side, or more if you like it well done. Swill out the pan with a little wine after you have taken out the meat, and pour it over it.

Rump steak in beer

you will need	1 − 1½ lb. rump steak
	2 tablespoons olive oil
	1 clove garlic
	salt and pepper
	½ pint beer
equipment	*grill pan*
	tablespoon
	sharp knife
	metal foil
	wooden spoon

Rub both sides of the steak with the olive oil, put it in the grill pan and sprinkle with the chopped garlic, salt, and freshly ground black pepper. Cover the pan with metal foil and leave for 1−2 hours.

Grill the steak to taste, remove from the pan and keep

hot. Pour the beer into the pan and stir well. Bring to the boil and pour over the steak. Serve with mashed or sauté potatoes, see page 178.

Sauerbraten

To serve 4 or more

you will need	salt and pepper
	grated nutmeg
	3 lb. topside
	1 large onion
	bay leaf
	1 tablespoon chopped parsley
	¼ pint vinegar
	¼ pint water
	2 oz. sugar
	2 oz. bacon fat
	2 tablespoons flour
	2 tablespoons evaporated milk
	2 oz. sultanas
equipment	*plastic container for meat*
	knife and chopping board
	saucepan and lid
	tablespoon

Rub salt and pepper and a little grated nutmeg into the joint. Make a marinade with the sliced onion, bay leaf, chopped parsley, vinegar, water and sugar. Bring them all to the boil, allow to cool a little, then pour them over the meat, which should be completely immersed. Leave overnight. As well as greatly improving the flavour of the meat, this marinade will ensure that it keeps well if you put it in the coolest place you can find.

Drain the meat, heat the bacon fat and brown the meat all over. Add about ¼ pint of the liquid to the pan, cover tightly and cook for 2 hours or until the meat is tender, adding more liquid as necessary. Thicken the gravy with the flour and milk and add the sultanas before serving.

Swiss steak

you will need	1½ lb. rump of fillet steak
	4 slices white bread
	salt and pepper
	4 slices Cheddar cheese
equipment	*mallet or rolling pin*
	grill pan
	board
	knife

Beat the steak well with a mallet or rolling pin to break down the fibres, then cut into 4 equal pieces. Grill lightly on one side then place cooked side down on the bread which should be slightly larger than the meat. Season to taste and grill the other side. Trim the bread to fit the meat, cover with the Cheddar cheese and grill until the cheese just starts to brown.

Steak rolls

To serve 4

you will need	1 onion
	4 rashers streaky bacon
	2 oz. mushrooms
	2 tablespoons olive oil
	1 lb. rump steak
	salt and pepper
	1 tablespoon chopped parsley
equipment	*knife and chopping board*
	large frying pan
	rolling pin or mallet
	tablespoon
	small bowl
	cotton or toothpicks

Chop the onion, bacon and mushrooms and fry until soft,

94

in the oil. Remove from the pan. While these are cooking, beat the steak well to break down the fibres and make it thinner. Cut into pieces about 4-inches × 2-inches, and spread some of the onion, bacon and mushroom mixture on each piece. Season and sprinkle with parsley. Roll up and secure. Fry all over until nicely browned and serve with potato croquettes, see page 179, omitting the cheese, and green beans.

Boeuf stroganoff

To serve 4

you will need	3 oz. butter
	2 onions
	4 oz. mushrooms
	3 tomatoes
	1 lb. fillet steak
	salt and pepper
	¼ pint sour cream
equipment	*frying pan*
	sharp knife and chopping board
	fish slice or spatula
	wooden spoon

Melt the butter in the frying pan and fry the chopped onions gently, until soft.

Remove from the pan and put in the sliced mushrooms, and when these are cooked take them out and fry the peeled and chopped tomatoes.

When these are soft take them out, raise the heat, and quickly fry the steak which you have cut into small thin strips against the grain. After 2—3 minutes return all the vegetables to the pan, add salt and pepper to taste and stir in the sour cream.

Serve with creamed potatoes and a green salad.

Cold salt beef

To serve 4 or more

you will need	2½ lb. lightly salted brisket, topside or silverside 1 onion 1 carrot 1 turnip few peppercorns
equipment	*large saucepan and lid* *knife and board*

Cover the meat with water and bring slowly to the boil. Skim well, then add the roughly chopped vegetables and the peppercorns. Simmer very gently for 2½ – 3 hours. Take out of the saucepan, put in a dish with a weighted plate on top and allow to become quite cold.

Save the stock for lentil soup, see next page.

Tomato mince

To serve 4

you will need	2 oz. dripping or lard 1 large onion 1 lb. minced beef 1 can peeled tomatoes 1 tablespoon tomato purée 1 tablespoon oatmeal salt 1 teaspoon paprika pinch cayenne pepper
equipment	*saucepan or frying pan with lid* *chopping board and knife*

Melt dripping and gently fry the finely chopped onion until tender. Add the meat and cook gently, stirring continuously, until brown. Pour in the canned tomatoes, and add the tomato purée, the oatmeal, salt to taste and the paprika and cayenne pepper. Cover and simmer gently for 20 – 30 minutes, stirring occasionally and adding a little water if it becomes too thick. Serve with toast or mashed potatoes.

Lentil soup

To serve 4 or more

you will need	2 carrots
	2 onions
	1 small turnip
	2 potatoes
	1 stick celery
	1 oz. dripping
	4 oz. lentils
	2 pints stock
	bouquet garni
	salt and pepper
equipment	*potato peeler*
	chopping board and knife
	large pan and lid
	wooden spoon
	sieve or liquidiser

Peel the carrots, onions, turnip and potatoes, and dice them with the celery. Fry them in the dripping, stirring from time to time. Add the lentils and continue to fry for a few more minutes. Add the stock. I always use the liquid from salt beef, see previous page which is excellent, and take both salt beef and lentil soup on most trips.

Add bouquet garni and season to taste, bring to the boil, cover the pan and simmer until the vegetables are tender.

Sieve or liquidise.

Topside in barbecue sauce

To serve 4

you will need	2 teaspoons dry mustard
	2 tablespoons wine vinegar
	3 tablespoons tomato purée
	2 tablespoons oil
	1 small chopped onion
	2 teaspoons brown sugar
	marjoram
	salt and pepper
	1 oz. dripping
	2 lb. topside
	2 onions
	2 carrots
	1 dessertspoon flour
equipment	*plastic beaker with lid*
	large saucepan and lid
	knife and board
	teaspoon
	tablespoon
	dessertspoon
	metal foil
	asbestos mat
	knife to carve the meat

Mix the mustard with the vinegar in the plastic beaker. Add the tomato purée, oil, chopped onion, brown sugar, marjoram, and salt and pepper, put the lid on the beaker and shake well.

Heat the dripping in the saucepan and brown the joint all over. Add the sliced carrots and quartered onions and the barbecue sauce, and see that the meat is well-coated with the sauce.

Put the lid on the saucepan, and if it doesn't fit too well seal it with metal foil, and cook for 1 – 1½ hours over a very low heat until the meat is tender. Thicken the liquid in the pan while someone carves the joint.

Any meat left over will make delicious sandwiches.

Beef pot roast

---

you will need	2 lb. topside or brisket
	olive oil
	dry mustard
	2 oz. dripping
	1 large onion
	salt and pepper
	herbs
	4 tablespoons water
equipment	*large saucepan and lid*
	knife and board
	tablespoon
	asbestos mat
	metal foil
	knife for carving
	wooden spoon

Rub the joint well with oil and dry mustard. Melt the dripping in the pan, and brown the joint all over. Add the sliced onion, sprinkle the joint with salt and pepper and a pinch of marjoram or sage. Pour the water in and put the lid on the pan. If the lid doesn't fit very well a circle of metal foil will keep the steam in.

Cook the joint, using the asbestos mat, on a very low heat for about 2½ hours or until the meat is tender. This may seem rather a long time for holiday cooking, but if the weather isn't too hot there is no reason why the joint shouldn't be started in the morning while the necessary chores are carried out, and finished in the evening.

When the meat is tender, get someone else to carve it while you pour off any surplus fat and thicken the remaining liquid with the flour to make the gravy.

Italian beef stew

you will need	1 clove garlic
	1 large onion
	2 tablespoons oil
	4 rashers streaky bacon
	1½ lb. chuck steak
	salt and pepper
	good pinch crushed rosemary
	½ pint cheap red wine
	2 tablespoons tomato purée
	1 teaspoon sugar
equipment	*knife and chopping board*
	saucepan and lid
	tablespoon
	teaspoon
	wooden spoon

Chop the garlic, slice the onion and fry until golden with the chopped bacon.

Cut the meat into ¾-inch cubes and add to the pan with salt and freshly ground black pepper to taste, and the marjoram and rosemary. Cook, stirring occasionally, until the meat is browned all over, then add the wine and cook until the wine is reduced a little.

Stir in the tomato purée and sugar and enough water to cover the meat.

Cover the pan and simmer until the meat is tender, about 1 – 1½ hours.

Adjust the seasoning and stir in a little more red wine before serving.

Beef paupiettes

you will need	1½ lb. chuck steak
	3 rashers streaky bacon
	2 slices white bread
	1 tablespoon made mustard
	1 onion, finely chopped
	2 oz. dripping or bacon fat
	1 tablespoon tomato purée
	¾ pint water
	1 teaspoon sugar
	salt and pepper
equipment	*large frying pan and lid*
	knife and chopping board
	tablespoon
	teaspoon
	measuring jug
	asbestos mat
	toothpicks

Ask the butcher to slice the steak into pieces about ¼-inch thick. Cut these into oblongs measuring about 4-inches × 1½-inches, and on each of these lay a piece of streaky bacon slightly smaller, and some onion. On top of each place a small piece of bread spread with the mustard, roll up and secure with a toothpick, or alternatively you could tie the rolls with cotton. Fry the rolls in the dripping until browned all over.

Mix the tomato purée, sugar and water in the jug, season to taste and add to the pan. Cook very gently for about 1 hour or until the beef is tender. Remove toothpicks before serving.

Braised steak and mushrooms

To serve 4

you will need	1½ lb. chuck steak
	2 tablespoons oil
	2 large onions
	4 oz. mushrooms
	1 tablespoon flour
	1 tablespoon tomato purée
	1 teaspoon sugar
	¼ pint stock or water
	salt and pepper
equipment	*knife and chopping board*
	large frying pan and lid
	tablespoon
	wooden spoon
	measuring jug
	teaspoon
	asbestos mat

Fry the steak in oil over a very hot flame until browned on both sides. Remove the meat from the pan. Lower the heat and fry the onions, sliced, and the mushrooms until soft, then stir in the flour and cook gently for a minute or two. Mix the tomato purée with the sugar and stock and add to the pan gradually, stirring all the time. Season to taste and bring to the boil, stirring.

Replace the meat and cook very gently, covered, for about 1½ hours, or until the steak is tender. Good with mashed potatoes, de-hydrated will do and French beans.

Lamb risotto

you will need	2 oz. mushrooms
	3 tomatoes
	3 tablespoons oil
	1½ lb. lean lamb of shoulder
	1 large onion
	6 oz. rice
	1 pint stock
	salt and pepper
	1 teaspoon marjoram
equipment	*knife and chopping board*
	cup for peeling tomatoes
	frying pan
	tablespoon
	wooden spoon
	teaspoon

Slice the mushrooms downwards, and pour boiling water on to the tomatoes to loosen skins. Heat the oil in the frying pan and fry the mushrooms and quartered tomatoes until soft.

Remove from the pan and then brown the meat which you have cut into 1-inch cubes. Stir in the chopped onion, fry for another 2 minutes, then add the rice and cook for 2 minutes more.

Add the stock, seasoning and marjoram, cover the pan and cook for about 20 minutes or until the rice is tender. By this time all the liquid should have been absorbed. Before serving stir in the mushrooms and tomatoes and heat through thoroughly.

Lamb fricassée

you will need	2½ lb. shoulder lamb
	salt and pepper
	marjoram
	2 large onions
	2 tablespoons olive oil
	yolks 2 eggs
	juice 1 lemon
	chopped parsley
equipment	*knife and chopping board*
	large frying pan with lid
	tablespoon
	wooden spoon
	fork and small bowl
	draining spoon

Cut the meat into small cubes, discarding most of the fat. Sprinkle with salt, pepper and marjoram.

Fry the sliced onions gently in the oil, add the meat and brown gently. Cover with ¾ pint water and simmer gently until the meat is tender, about 50 minutes.

Whisk together egg yolks and lemon juice. Remove tne meat from the pan, add egg and lemon mixture and stir over a low heat until thick.

Put the meat back to heat through and sprinkle with chopped parsley.

Good with mashed potatoes and glazed carrots, see page 171.

Navarin of lamb

you will need	1½ – 2 lb. middle neck of lamb
	1 tablespoon lard
	2 onions
	2 carrots
	1 small turnip
	1 teaspoon sugar
	1 tablespoon flour
	1 pint water or stock
	salt and pepper
	1 pinch marjoram
	chopped parsley
equipment	*knife and chopping board*
	large frying pan and lid
	tablespoon
	teaspoon
	wooden spoon
	asbestos mat

Cut off some of the fat from the lamb and brown the meat all over in the lard. Remove it from the pan and put in the sliced vegetables. Dust them with the sugar and fry gently until they are coloured, stirring from time to time. Stir in the flour and cook for a few minutes, then add the stock a little at a time and bring to the boil, stirring all the time. Lower the heat and replace the meat. Add the seasoning and herbs, cover the pan and cook very gently, the liquid should just move now and then, for 30 minutes. Turn the meat and cook for a further 30 minutes.

Lamb and apricots with dumplings

To serve 4

you will need	1½ lb. best end of neck
	1 oz. dripping
	½ lb. dried apricots
	1 tablespoon lemon juice
	1 teaspoon thyme
	salt and pepper
	4 oz. self-raising flour
	2 oz. shredded suet
equipment	*knife and chopping board*
	frying pan
	slice or spatula
	knife
	saucepan and lid
	tablespoon
	teaspoon
	bowl and blunt knife

Trim some of the fat away from the lamb and brown in the dripping on both sides. Soak the apricots for 2 hours in enough water to cover.

Put the browned meat into the saucepan, just cover with water, add lemon juice, thyme and salt and pepper to taste.

Bring to the boil and simmer gently for 30 minutes, then add the apricots and the water in which they have been soaking. Simmer for another hour.

Put the flour and suet in the bowl with a good pinch of salt and add enough water to make a stiff dough. Form into small dumplings, drop into the pan, put the lid on firmly and continue to cook fairly fast for another 15 minutes.

Celebration lamb curry

To serve 4

you will need	2 lb. boned shoulder lamb
	1 small onion
	1 clove garlic
	1 oz. mutton fat or lard
	good pinch round ginger
	$\frac{1}{2}$ level teaspoon salt
	3 level dessertspoons curry powder
	1 good orange
	1 level dessertspoon cornflour
equipment	*knife and chopping board*
	saucepan and lid
	dessertspoon
	teaspoon
	wooden spoon
	lemon squeezer
	measuring jug

Remove all the fat from the lamb and cut it into 1-inch cubes. Chop the onion and garlic finely. Fry the lamb in the fat until well browned on all sides, then add the onion and garlic and cook for a few minutes more. Drain off all the fat.

Stir in the ginger, salt and curry powder. This quantity will give rather a hot curry so add half at a time and taste it. Squeeze the orange and make the juice up to $\frac{1}{2}$ pint with water.

Add to the meat, bring to the boil and simmer very gently for about 1 hour or until the lamb is tender. Blend the cornflour with a little water, add to the pan, stir well and bring to the boil.

Serve with orange rice, see page 110 and several side dishes, see page 165.

Lamb with prunes and
almonds

you will need
    ½ lb. prunes
2 lb. shoulder of lamb
2 onions
salt and pepper
pinch marjoram
juice 1 lemon
2 oz. butter
1 tablespoon flour
¾ pint stock or water
8 oz. blanched almonds
teaspoon sugar
boiled rice, see page 110

equipment
    small bowl or jug
larger bowl or saucepan
chopping board
sharp knife
lemon squeezer
tablespoon
wooden spoon
teaspoon
second saucepan

Soak the prunes over night. Cut the meat into 1-inch cubes,
discarding some of the fat, and put into the large bowl
with the sliced onions, salt and pepper, marjoram and lemon
juice. Leave for at least an hour, longer if possible. Drain
the meat and onions and fry lightly in the butter, then stir
in the flour and fry for a few minutes. Add the stock, bring
to the boil, stirring, then simmer over a gentle heat for
about 45 minutes.

Add the prunes and almonds and cook until the prunes
are tender, stir in a little sugar and the lemon juice, bring to
the boil once more and serve with the boiled rice.

Savoury lamb chops   To serve 4

you will need	4 chump chops
	1 oz. butter
	2 onions, chopped
	salt and pepper
	1 tablespoon chopped parsley
	4 level tablespoons breadcrumbs
equipment	*frying pan and lid*
	knife and chopping board
	tablespoon

Fry the chops in the butter until brown on both sides. Remove from the pan and put in the chopped onion. Replace chops on top. Season to taste, cover the pan and cook slowly for 25 – 30 minutes, until the chops are tender. Sprinkle parsley and breadcrumbs over the chops, baste with some of the fat and put under a hot grill until nicely brown.

Good with tinned tomatoes and creamed potatoes.

Lamb with mushrooms   To serve 4

you will need	12 – 16 thin slices lamb
	4 oz. mushrooms
	2 teaspoons chopped parsley
	3 oz. butter
	1 tablespoon flour
	½ pint Béchamel sauce, see page 185
equipment	*shallow bowl*
	frying pan

Soak slices of meat in hot water. Cook mushrooms and parsley in the butter. Remove meat slices from water and dust them with flour. Add these to cooked mushrooms and butter. Cook for about 10 minutes. Stir together. Pour over the freshly made sauce.

Orange rice

you will need	2 oz. butter
	1 large onion
	2 oranges
	6 oz. long grain rice
	level teaspoon salt
equipment	*knife and chopping board*
	saucepan and lid
	orange squeezer
	teaspoon
	wooden spoon
	measuring jug

Melt the butter in the pan and fry the chopped onion until soft. Pare the rind of the oranges very thinly, taking great care not to cut the pith, chop it and add to the pan. Stir in the rice and cook gently for 3—4 minutes. Squeeze orange and make up the juice to ¾ pint with water. Add it to the rice, bring to the boil, cover the pan and simmer for about 20 minutes. Peel and slice the other orange, cut into quarters and stir into the rice.

Boiled rice

To serve 4

you will need	¾ pint water
	1 level teaspoon salt
	6 oz. long grain rice
equipment	*measuring jug*
	teaspoon
	saucepan and lid
	fork

Put the water into the saucepan and bring to the boil. Add the salt and the rice, stir and bring back to the boil. Cover the pan tightly, reduce the heat and cook for 15 minutes, when the rice should be cooked and all the water absorbed.

Pilaff

To serve 4

you will need	8 oz. rice
	2 tomatoes
	2 oz. mushrooms
	½ sweet green pepper
	2 oz. butter
equipment	*knife and chopping board*
	saucepan and lid
	small bowl or jug
	frying pan
	fork

Prepare the rice in the normal way, see previous recipe. Fry the peeled and quartered tomatoes, the sliced mushrooms and the de-seeded, chopped sweet pepper in the butter, and when they are all cooked mix the cooked rice in thoroughly with a fork.

Variation

To make a Plain Turkish or Greek Pilaff you need 8 oz. rice, 2 pints of meat stock, 1 teaspoon salt, 3 oz. dripping or butter, 1 teaspoon black pepper, 2 oz. melted butter.

Melt the fat in a large pot, add the rice and fry for 5 minutes. Boil the stock and when boiling pour on to the frying rice; add salt and pepper. Cover the pot with a clean cloth and then clamp on the lid. Cook on a very low heat until there is no liquid left (about 50 minutes). Remove from heat, still covered, and stand for 20 minutes. Pour the melted butter over and mix well before eating.

Braised pork chops

you will need	1 tablespoon olive oil
	4 good loin chops
	salt and pepper
	1 dessertspoon flour
	½ pint milk
equipment	*large frying pan and lid*
	tablespoon
	fish slice
	dessertspoon
	asbestos mat

Heat the oil in the frying pan until very hot. Brown the chops on both sides. Lower the heat, season to taste, cover the pan and cook for 30 or 40 minutes or until the chops are tender. Take the chops out of the pan, stir in the flour, add the milk gradually and bring to the boil. Put the chops back to heat through. Serve with potato croquettes, omitting cheese, see page 179, apple sauce and a green vegetable.

Pork chops with barbecue sauce

To serve 4

you will need	little olive oil
	4 loin chops
	salt and pepper
	barbecue sauce 2, see page 193
	watercress
equipment	*large frying pan with lid*
	asbestos mat

Heat the oil and fry the chops quickly until browned on both sides. Season. Make the barbecue sauce in the pan after you have removed the chops, using the fat that has run out of them, bring to the boil and simmer, stirring, for 2—3 minutes.

Replace the chops, lower the heat, cover, and cook slowly for about 20 minutes or until the chops are tender. Serve garnished with the watercress.

Spanish pork chops   To serve 4

you will need	4 good pork chops
	1 oz. dripping
	1 large onion
	1 small can tomatoes
	salt and pepper
	1 tablespoon flour
equipment	*knife and chopping board*
	large frying pan and lid
	can opener
	wooden spoon
	tablespoon

Brown chops slowly on both sides in the dripping. Take the chops out of the pan and cook the onions until soft. Replace chops, add the tomatoes and season to taste. Cover and cook slowly for about 30 minutes, until the chops are tender.

Remove the meat, thicken the sauce with the flour and put the chops back to get piping hot again.

Serve with boiled rice, see page 110.

Variation

For Madrid pork chops: brown the chops in 4 tablespoons of olive oil. Then add 2 cloves of garlic, chopped; tablespoon of chopped parsley; a bay leaf; a sliced chilli pepper; ½ teaspoon marjoram. Cover the pan. Turn the chops from time to time so the herbs can penetrate both sides.

113

Sauté of pork

To serve **4**

you will need
1 medium-sized onion
1 — 1½ lb. pork fillet
1 oz. butter
2 oz. mushrooms
1 level tablespoon flour
2 teaspoons paprika
salt
¼ pint sherry
¼ pint stock
¼ pint thin cream or top of the milk

equipment
knife and chopping board
large frying pan and lid
teaspoon
tablespoon
wooden spoon
measuring jug

Chop the onion and slice the pork. Sauté them both in butter, then add the sliced mushrooms and cook for another 2 — 3 minutes.

Stir in the flour and paprika and salt to taste, add the sherry and stock gradually, stirring, and bring to the boil. Lower the heat and simmer very gently for about 40 minutes or until the pork is tender.

Stir in the cream or top of the milk and serve with mashed potatoes or boiled rice, see page 110.

Variation

Cut the pork into thin strips. Fry in the butter with the chopped onion for 5 minutes. Add 1 lb. green beans, fesh or frozen, and toss together for 5 — 6 minutes more. Pour in a tablespoon of soy sauce and season with pepper. Serve very hot. Delicious with boiled of fried rice or noodles.

Blanquette de veau

you will need	1½ lb. boneless veal
	8 oz. small onions
	4 oz. button mushrooms
	2 oz. butter
	1 pint stock
	chopped parsley
	2 bay leaves
	2 oz. flour
	2 tablespoons cream
	1 egg yolk
	salt and pepper
equipment	*knife and chopping board*
	saucepan and lid
	measuring jug
	fork
	wooden spoon
	tablespoon

Cut the veal into cubes, peel the onions and wash the mushrooms. Fry them all in the butter for a few minutes until they are all well coated. Add the stock and herbs, cover the saucepen and cook very gently for about 1½ hours or until the veal is tender.

Mix togehter the flour, cream and egg yolk and add a little of the stock, stirring until smooth. Remove the bay leaf from the pan and stir in the egg yolk mixture, heating through but not allowing to come to the boil again. Season to taste.

Serve with mashed potatoes or noodles.

Western Isle veal

you will need	2 tablespoons olive oil
	1¼ lb. fillet veal
	1 large onion
	1 clove garlic
	1 small can tomatoes
	1 teaspoon sugar
	salt and pepper
	¼ pint dry white wine
	marjoram
	few drops tabasco sauce
equipment	*knife and chopping board*
	large frying pan and lid
	tablespoon
	tin opener
	asbestos mat

Heat the oil in the frying pan and fry the veal until golden brown.

Remove from the pan and put in the chopped onion and garlic and cook until soft.

Stir in the tomatoes, sugar, salt and pepper to taste, the wine, a pinch of marjoram and a few drops of tabasco.

Stir well, put the veal back, and cook over the lowest possible heat for about an hour.

Veal chops bonne femme

you will need	4 veal chops
	2 oz. butter
	12 shallots
	4 oz. bacon
	4 oz. mushrooms
	1 tablespoon flour
	$\frac{3}{4}$ pint stock
	salt and pepper
	$1\frac{1}{2}$ lb. potatoes
	chopped parsley
equipment	*knife and chopping board*
	large frying pan and lid
	potato peeler
	tablespoon
	wooden spoon
	asbestos mat

Brown the chops well in the butter. Remove them from the pan, and fry the shallots, chopped bacon and sliced mushrooms. When they are soft, stir in the flour, and then the stock a little at a time. Season, replace the chops, and simmer very gently for about 20 minutes. Now add the peeled potatoes to the pan, cut to the size of about half an egg. Cook very slowly for another 20 minutes, or until both potatoes and meat are tender, and serve garnished with plenty of chopped parsley.

Breaded veal chops

you will need	4 large veal chops
	1 egg
	2 tablespoons milk
	1 packet breadcrumbs
	2 oz. butter
	1 onion
	1 sweet green pepper
	$\frac{1}{2}$ pint stock or water
	salt and pepper
equipment	*knife and chopping board*
	large frying pan and lid
	2 plates
	cup for egg and milk
	fork
	knife and board
	wooden spoon

Dip chops first in beaten egg and milk, then in breadcrumbs. Fry until golden brown in the butter.

Remove from the pan and fry the de-seeded, chopped sweet pepper with the chopped onion. Replace veal, add stock or water, season to taste. Cover the pan and cook slowly for about 1 hour.

If too liquid towards the end of the cooking time, take the lid off for the last 10 minutes.

Creole ragoût

you will need	3 rashers streaky bacon
	1½ lb. leg or shoulder veal
	1 oz. butter
	1 tablespoon olive oil
	2 onions
	1 clove garlic
	1 level dessertspoon flour
	1 teaspoon tomato purée
	½ pint stock
	teaspoon mixed dried herbs
	salt and pepper
equipment	*knife and chopping board*
	large frying pan and lid
	tablespoon
	dessertspoon
	teaspoon
	wooden spoon
	asbestos mat

Chop the bacon and cut the veal into 1-inch cubes. Brown these in the oil and butter, lower the heat and add the sliced onions and chopped garlic. Cook together until the onion is soft, then stir in the flour and remove from the heat. Mix together the tomato purée, stock and herbs, add to the pan and bring to the boil. Season to taste and cook very gently for about 45 minutes or until the veal is tender.

Veal escalopes with orange

To serve 4

you will need	4 good escalopes
	2 oz. butter
	1 dessertspoon flour
	2 oranges
	small glass of sherry
	¼ pint stock
	salt and pepper
	parsley
equipment	*large frying pan and lid*
	dessertspoon
	lemon squeezer
	grater
	small glass
	wooden spoon
	small jug or bowl
	sharp knife and board

Fry the escalopes in the butter until golden brown. Take out the meat, stir in the flour and grate the rind of 1 orange into the pan. Add the juice of 1 orange, the sherry and the stock.

Replace the escalopes, season to taste, and bring very slowly to the boil, then cover the pan and simmer very gently for about 15 minutes or until the escalopes are tender.

While the escalopes are cooking, pour boiling water on to the other orange, leave for 1 minute and then peel.

Cut from it 4 slices and serve one on each escalope, spooning the sauce over and sprinkling it all with the chopped parsley.

Veal à la king

To serve 4

you will need	1½ lb. stewing veal
	1 level teaspoon salt
	2 good sticks celery
	½ sweet green pepper
	2 oz. butter
	2 tablespoons flour
	about 2 tablespoons thin cream or evaporated milk
	2 hard-boiled eggs
	salt and pepper
equipment	*sharp knife*
	chopping board
	large pan and lid
	measuring jug
	tablespoon
	wooden spoon
	asbestos mat

Cut the veal in 1-inch cubes, add salt and enough water to cover, bring to the boil and simmer very gently for 1 hour or until the meat is tender. Remove the meat from the pan and pour the stock into the measuring jug. Rinse out the pan and fry the chopped celery and the de-seeded, chopped pepper in the butter until soft. Stir in the flour. Make the stock up to a generous ½ pint with water if necessary, then stir this into the pan and add the cream, starting with about 2 tablespoons and adding more if the sauce is too thick. Cook over a moderate heat, stirring all the time, until the sauce boils. Add the meat and the chopped hard-boiled eggs. Serve with fresh tomatoes.

Broad beans and devilled bacon

To serve **4**

you will need	8 rashers bacon
	1 level tablespoon dry mustard
	few drops vinegar
	few drops Worcestershire or tabasco sauce
	4 tomatoes
	1 large can broad beans
	milk
	1 oz. margarine or butter
	1 oz. flour
	salt and pepper
equipment	*knife and board*
	measuring jug
	tablespoon
	teaspoon
	can opener
	wooden spoon
	grill pan
	saucepan

Remove rind from bacon. Mix mustard with vinegar and a few drops of the sauce to a spreading consistency. Spread the mixture on the bacon and grill. Grill tomatoes. In the meantime, strain the liquor from the broad beans and make up to ½ pint with milk. Melt the margarine or butter in the saucepan, stir in the flour and gradually add the liquid, stirring all the time. Season. Bring to the boil and stir in the broad beans and heat through. Dish on to plates and top with bacon and tomatoes.

Sweet pepper and bacon risotto

To serve 2

you will need	8 oz. back bacon, thickly cut
	1 onion
	1 oz. margarine
	½ sweet green pepper
	4 oz. rice
	1 tablespoon tomato purée
	½ pint water
	salt and pepper
	1 teaspoon sugar
	1 tablespoon chopped parsley
	grated cheese
equipment	*knife and board*
	frying pan
	tablespoon
	teaspoon
	wooden spoon

Fry the chopped bacon and onion in the melted fat for 2 – 3 minutes.

Add the finely sliced sweet pepper, then stir in the rice and cook for another 3 minutes until all the fat has been absorbed.

Stir in the tomato purée, water, salt and pepper to taste and sugar and chopped parsley. Bring to the boil, then simmer gently until the liquid has been absorbed and the rice is tender, which should take about 20 minutes.

Serve sprinkled with grated cheese.

Braised ham with bananas

To serve 4

you will need	1 oz. butter
	4 thick gammon steaks
	2 bananas
	4 tablespoons coconut
	2 tablespoons lemon juice
	3 oz. soft brown sugar
equipment	*sharp knife and board*
	large frying pan and lid
	tablespoon

Melt the butter in the frying pan and put in the trimmed gammon steaks. Slice the bananas on to the gammon, sprinkle with the coconut and add the lemon juice and brown sugar. Cook very gently for about 25 minutes.

Grilled gammon with honey

To serve 4

you will need	4 good gammon rashers
	1 dessertspoon dry mustard
	3 tablespoons honey
	1 tablespoon white wine
equipment	*knife and board*
	tablespoon
	dessertspoon
	jug
	grill pan

Cut the rind from the gammon and make slits all the way round to prevent the fat from curling up and burning.

Mix the mustard with the honey and rub the mixture into each rasher.

Then mix in the wine and baste the gammon with this as it grills.

Good served with potato croquettes and a crisp green salad.

Gammon braised with aubergine

To serve 4

you will need	1 large onion
	1 tablespoon olive oil
	1 aubergine
	1½ level tablespoons flour
	¼ pint water
	1 tablespoon lemon juice or vinegar
	1 teaspoon soy sauce
	pepper and salt
	1 lb. gammon ½-inch thick
equipment	*knife and chopping board*
	large pan and lid
	tablespoon
	teaspoon
	wooden spoon

Fry the chopped onion in the oil for 2 minutes. Peel and slice the aubergine and add to the pan. Mix together the flour, water, lemon juice or vinegar, soy sauce, pepper and a very little salt and add to the pan.

Dice the gammon and add, bring to the boil, stirring, cover the pan and simmer very gently for about 30 minutes or until the gammon is tender.

Serve with creamed potatoes or boiled rice, see page 110.

125

Gammon and pineapple

To serve 4

you will need	4 gammon steaks
	little olive oil
	1 medium-sized can pineapple rings
	4 firm tomatoes
equipment	*sharp knife and board*
	pastry brush
	grill pan
	can opener

Remove the rind from the gammon and slash the fat at ½-inch intervals to prevent curling when grilled. Brush on both sides with olive oil, grill and serve garnished with a ring of pineapple on each rasher and a half tomato in each ring.

Good and very attractive to look at served with sauté potatoes and green peas.

Cowboys' supper

To serve 4

you will need	12 thin rashers short back bacon
	1 large can baked beans
	2 hard-boiled eggs
	salt and pepper
equipment	*knife and board*
	frying pan
	slice
	can opener

Remove rind from bacon and fry quickly in a hot dry frying pan. Keep warm, and heat the beans until bubbling

126

in the bacon fat. Dish the bacon on top of the beans and garnish with the hard-boiled eggs. Season to taste.

Serve with rolls and butter.

West Indian chop suey To serve 4

you will need	8 thick rashers bacon
	1 tablespoon oil
	1 onion
	4 stalks celery
	1 sweet green pepper
	salt and pepper
equipment	*knife and chopping board*
	frying pan and lid
	tablespoon
	wooden spoon

Chop bacon finely and cook in the oil until the fat begins to melt.

Chop the onion and the celery and de-seed and slice the sweet pepper.

Add to the pan, increase the heat and fry quickly, stirring from time to time, until the vegetables are tender. Season and serve.

Variations

1. Instead of celery and pepper, add a finely chopped cabbage and 4 sliced tomatoes to the bacon and onion. Season well.
2. Or add about 1 lb. green beans, fresh or frozen, and 4 sliced tomatoes to the pan and cook until tender. Then a chopped hard-boiled egg.

Cheesy ham rolls

you will need	4 good heads chicory
	lemon juice
	1 oz. butter
	1 oz. flour
	4 oz. grated cheese
	½ pint milk
	salt and pepper
	8 oz. sliced ham
equipment	*knife*
	saucepan and lid
	tin or dish for serving
	jug and fork for dried milk
	wooden spoon
	grater or potato peeler
	small pan for sauce

Remove any discoloured leaves from chicory and boil in salted water with a squeeze of lemon juice. Meanwhile, pour some very hot water into your serving dish.

Melt the butter in the small saucepan, stir in the flour, then gradually add the milk, which can be fresh, evaporated or reconstituted dried milk. Stir all the time to keep the sauce smooth, then add the grated cheese and salt and pepper to taste. If the chicory is not ready when you have made the sauce, put a plate over the small saucepan to prevent a skin from forming.

When the chicory is tender, whip it out of the pan, drain it, wrap a slice of ham round each head and put it in the warmed dish. Pour the cheese sauce on, and if you have a grill sprinkle a little more cheese on top and brown it.

Delicious eaten with wholemeal bread and butter and firm red tomatoes.

Variation:

Leeks or cauliflower can be used instead of chicory.

Calves' liver with orange

To serve 4

you will need	2 oz. butter
	1¼ lb. calves' liver
	2 tablespoons flour
	salt and pepper
	1 teaspoon dry mustard
	1 onion
	1 clove garlic
	2 tablespoons red wine
	½ pint stock
	1 orange
equipment	*sharp knife and board*
	frying pan
	plate
	tablespoon
	teaspoon
	wooden spoon
	measuring jug

Heat the butter in the frying pan, and roll the sliced liver in the flour, salt and pepper and mustard. Brown it quickly on both sides and remove from the pan. Fry the chopped onion and garlic until soft, add the wine and cook quickly until reduced a little. Stir in the stock and bring to the boil, stirring all the time. Put the liver back in the pan to heat through.

Meanwhile, pour boiling water on to the orange to loosen the skin, peel and slice it and use as a garnish for the liver.

Variation

If you have a grill cut the orange into thin slices, brush with olive oil and sprinkle it with brown sugar, and brown quickly under the grill on top of the liver. Serve with cauliflower and mashed or sauté potatoes.

Liver hot pot

you will need	4 oz. mushrooms
	4 rashers streaky bacon
	1 large onion
	2 tablespoons oil
	salt and pepper
	1¼ lb. lamb's liver
	1 small can tomatoes
	1 teaspoon sugar
	1 tablespoon chopped parsley
equipment	*knife and chopping board*
	large frying pan and lid
	tablespoon
	wooden spoon
	can opener
	teaspoon

Chop the mushrooms, bacon and onion and fry in the oil until tender. Season to taste, then push to one side and lay the thinly sliced liver in the pan. Heap the onion mixture on top of the liver, add the tomatoes and sugar and bring gently to the boil. Cover the pan and cook slowly for 5 minutes, or more if you like your liver well done.

Sprinkle with chopped parsley and serve with mashed potatoes or boiled rice, see page 110.

Variation

Slice 1 lb. potatoes thinly. Then lightly fry the onion, bacon and sliced liver. Cook about 1 oz. of flour in the pan and then stir in ¾ pint stock. Put a layer of sliced potatoes in a casserole or saucepan, then a layer of liver, bacon, onion and tomatoes. Alternate these layers, seasoning them well, ending with a layer of potatoes. Pour in the stock. Cook very slowly in a saucepan until potatoes are cooked.

Ragoût of pig's kidneys

To serve 4

you will need	4 pigs' kidneys
	1 large onion
	6 oz. mushrooms
	1 oz. dripping
	salt and pepper to taste
	1 teaspoon marjoram
	1 teaspoon tomato purée
	good pinch sugar
	1 level tablespoon flour
	½ pint stock
	chopped parsley
equipment	*knife and chopping board*
	saucepan and lid
	teaspoon
	tablespoon
	wooden spoon
	measuring jug

Soak the kidneys for 1 – 2 hours if possible. Remove the cores and chop roughly. Slice the onion and the mushrooms and fry all together in the dripping. Add salt and pepper to taste and the marjoram.

Stir in the tomato purée, sugar and flour, then add the stock gradually, stirring all the time. Bring slowly to the boil, stirring.

Lower the heat and cook gently for about 20 minutes, or until the kidneys are tender. Add more stock if the liquid gets too thick.

Sprinkle with chopped parsley and serve with boiled rice, see page 110.

Devilled kidneys

you will need	1½ lb. veal kidneys
	2 oz. butter
	salt and pepper
	1 dessertspoon flour
	¼ pint stock or white wine
	1 teaspoon made mustard
	1 teaspoon chopped parsley
	squeeze lemon juice
equipment	*knife and board*
	frying pan and lid
	dessertspoon
	teaspoon
	wooden spoon

Skin the kidneys and fry in the butter until browned all over. Add salt and pepper to taste, cover the pan, and cook gently for about 10 minutes or until the kidneys are tender.

Remove the kidneys from the pan and slice. Stir in the flour, then the stock or wine, and bring to the boil.

Add the mustard, parsley and lemon juice and stir well. Return the kidneys to the pan and bring to boiling point once more.

Serve with mashed potatoes and green beans.

Variation

Stir in 1 teaspoon of curry powder with the flour, before adding the stock to the pan.

Then add 1 tablespoon of chutney when the kidneys are returned to the pan.

Put the kidney mixture in the centre of a border of mashed potatoes, and garnish with 2 sliced, hard-boiled eggs.

Sauté of kidneys and mushrooms

To serve 4

you will need	8 oz. mushrooms
	1 small onion
	1 clove garlic
	3 oz. butter
	1½ lb. lambs' kidneys
	salt
	freshly ground black pepper
	1 tablespoon flour
	½ pint stock
	¼ pint white wine
	small can evaporated milk
	chopped parsley
equipment	*sharp knife*
	chopping board
	large frying pan and lid
	can opener
	wooden spoon
	tablespoon

Wash and slice the mushrooms, chop the onion and the garlic.

Fry gently in 1 oz. of butter and remove from the pan. Add remainder of the butter and fry the sliced kidneys for a few minutes.

Return mushrooms and onions to the pan, season to taste and stir in the flour.

Slowly add the stock, wine and evaporated milk. Bring to the boil, stirring all the time. Cover and simmer very gently for 15 minutes.

Adjust seasoning and sprinkle with chopped parsley before serving.

Mixed grill

you will need	lamb cutlets
	lamb's liver
	sausages
	short back bacon
	4 tomatoes
	kidney
	8 oz. mushrooms
	potato crisps
	watercress
	olive oil
equipment	*sharp knife and board*
	grill pan
	pastry brush
	frying pan

Personally if I were serving a mixed grill for 4 on 2 burners and a grill I should cheat a bit and fry the sausage, liver, tomatoes and mushrooms. Or better still turn it all into kebabs, see page 35 and let everyone cook their own over an open fire beneath the stars.

Variation

There is no reason why veal or pork chops, or cutlets could not be used instead of lamb, but a lamb chop is the most general choice. The secret of a good mixed grill is to time the cooking carefully, i.e. do not put all the items under the grill at the same time; start with food that takes the longest cooking, then gradually add other ingredients. Do make sure grill is really hot before cooking and keep kidneys, steak and liver well basted with butter. Remember kidneys are easily over-cooked, so add these towards the end. Sausages on the other hand require a fair amount of cooking.

Pork sausages and Danish potato salad

To serve 4

you will need	12 plump pork sausages
	1 oz. butter
	1½ lb. potatoes
	2 large onions
	4 cooking apples
	½ teaspoon sugar
	salt and pepper
	1 tablespoon wine vinegar
equipment	*knife and chopping board*
	large frying pan and lid
	saucepan and lid
	potato peeler
	teaspoon
	tablespoon
	wooden spoon

Prick the sausages all over and fry them gently in the butter. Peel the potatoes and cook them whole until they are tender but still whole. Slice.

Remove the sausages from the pan when they are nicely browned, and fry the sliced onions until soft. Add the peeled and quartered apple and cook for 2−3 minutes, then add the sliced potatoes and the sugar, stir gently and season to taste. Sprinkle the vinegar over, return to the pan the cooked sausages and serve as soon as it is all really hot.

Spanish sausage

you will need	1½ lb. pork sausage meat
	scant tablespoon oil
	½ sweet green pepper
	1 onion
	2 sticks celery
	1 small can tomatoes
	1 level teaspoon sugar
	salt and pepper
	1 tablespoon flour
	¼ pint water
	grated Parmesan cheese
equipment	*knife and chopping board*
	large frying pan and lid
	tablespoon
	teaspoon
	wooden spoon
	can opener
	measuring jug

Form the sausage meat into 10 or 12 patties and brown on both sides in the oil.

Pour away about half the fat in the pan. Remove the seeds from the sweet pepper, and chop it with the onion and the celery.

Add to the pan and fry gently until soft. Stir in the tomatoes, sugar and salt and pepper to taste. Cover the pan and cook very slowly for about 30 minutes, or until the sausage is cooked through. Blend the flour and water.

Remove the sausage patties from the pan and keep warm, stir in the flour paste and bring to the boil, stirring all the time. Serve over the patties and sprinkle with Parmesan cheese.

Chicken Maryland

you will need	1 young chicken
	1 beaten egg
	breadcrumbs
	2 oz. butter
	4 tomatoes
	salt and pepper
	1 oz. flour
	¼ pint milk
	¼ pint chicken stock
	1 medium-sized can sweet corn
	2 bananas
equipment	*large frying pan and lid*
	fork
	jug
	knife
	can opener
	wooden spoon
	saucepan for sweet corn

Cut the chicken into serving pieces, or ask the butcher to do it for you.

Dip each piece into beaten egg, then into bread crumbs, and fry until golden brown.

Cover the pan and cook very slowly until tender, then remove the chicken and fry the tomatoes until soft but still whole. When they are cooked keep them warm while you stir the flour into the fat and add the milk and stock to make a smooth sauce. Season. Return the chicken to the pan and coat all over with the sauce and make very hot.

Meanwhile heat the sweet corn and slice the bananas and serve it all together.

Chicken sauté Espagnol

To serve 4

you will need	2½ lb. roasting chicken
	2 tablespoons oil
	1 large onion
	1 clove garlic
	¼ pint sherry
	1 level tablespoon flour
	¼ pint chicken stock
	1 small can tomatoes
	1 teaspoon sugar
	salt and pepper
	chopped parsley
equipment	*knife and chopping board*
	large frying pan and lid
	tablespoon
	teaspoon
	wooden spoon
	measuring jug
	can opener
	asbestos mat

Ask the butcher to joint the chicken for you. Heat the oil, brown the chicken pieces carefully all over and remove from the pan. Chop the onion and garlic finely and fry gently until soft, then add the sherry to the pan and increase the heat.

Cook until the sherry has evaporated, then stir in the flour, then the stock, tomatoes and seasonings.
Stir until boiling.

Replace the chicken joints, cover the pan and simmer very gently for 25 minutes, or until the chicken is tender.

Serve sprinkled with chopped parsley.

Normandy chicken

you will need	2½ lb. roasting chicken
	1 tablespoon oil
	1 oz. butter
	2 dessert apples
	1 clove garlic
	1 onion
	salt and pepper
	1 level tablespoon flour
	1 teaspoon mixed herbs
	¼ pint sherry or cider
	½ pint chicken stock
	1 tablespoon cream
	chopped parsley
equipment	*knife and chopping board*
	large frying pan and lid
	tablespoon
	teaspoon
	wooden spoon
	measuring jug

Cut the chicken into serving pieces or ask the butcher to do it for you. Heat the oil and butter and fry the chicken until golden brown. Remove from the pan. Cut the peeled apples into slices and fry gently until soft but still whole and remove these. Now fry the garlic and onion until soft, season to taste, stir in the flour and then add the herbs. Gradually add the sherry or cider and chicken stock and bring to the boil, stirring all the time.

Replace the chicken joints, lower the heat and cover the pan. Cook very gently, basting occasionally, for about 20 minutes, or until the chicken is tender.

Dish up the chicken, quickly stir in the cream and pour it all over the joints. Sprinkle with chopped parsley.

Lemon chicken

you will need	1 frying chicken
	2 tablespoons olive oil
	salt and pepper
	2 lemons
equipment	*knife*
	large frying pan and lid
	tablespoon
	lemon squeezer
	asbestos mat

Cut the chicken into serving pieces, or ask the butcher to do it for you.

Brown the pieces all over in the oil. Dust each piece with salt and pepper, pour the lemon juice over and bring to the boil.

Lower the heat, cover the pan and cook very slowly for 45 minutes or until the chicken is tender.

Serve with French bread and Normandy butter and lots of green salad.

Variation

Use a jointed boiling fowl, and after squeezing the lemon juice over it put it into a saucepan with diced vegetables that include: 8 oz. onions, 8 oz. carrots, a few sticks of celery; together with 2 bay leaves and 3 white peppercorns. Add water to one inch of the top and season. Cook for 1½ hours in a saucepan over a slow heat. When tender remove chicken and keep warm. Fry 4 oz. sliced mushrooms in 2 oz. butter. Beat 1 egg and 4 tablespoons cream together and gradually add ½ pint of the hot stock, stirring all the time until smooth and thick. Add the mushrooms, ¼ pint sherry and 4 oz. blanched almonds. Replace the chicken and surround with sauce.

MAIN DISHES USING CANS

Hungarian goulash

To serve 4

you will need	1 sweet green pepper
	1 onion
	1 tablespoon olive oil
	1 lb. potatoes
	1 small can tomatoes
	2 teaspoons paprika
	1 teaspoon sugar
	salt and pepper
	1 large can braised steak
	2 teaspoons cornflour
equipment	*knife and board*
	tablespoon
	large saucepan and lid
	can opener
	potato peeler
	teaspoon
	wooden spoon

De-seed the pepper and slice it. Fry it with the chopped onion in the oil for 3 – 4 minutes. Add the peeled and halved potatoes to the pan with the canned tomatoes, stir in the paprika, sugar and seasoning to taste and bring to the boil. Simmer very gently for about 10 minutes. Add the braised steak and simmer for another 10 minutes or until the potatoes are tender. Thicken with the cornflour if necessary.

If liked, omit the potatoes, cook for only 10 minutes and serve with boiled rice, see page 110.

Beef stew with dumplings

To serve 4

you will need	2 rashers streaky bacon
	1 clove garlic
	1 large onion
	4 oz. mushrooms
	1 large can braised steak
	3 teaspoons tomato purée
	salt and pepper
	1 level teaspoon sugar
	4 oz. flour
	2 oz. shredded suet
	tablespoon chopped parsley
equipment	*knife and chopping board*
	large saucepan and lid
	can opener
	teaspoon
	tablespoon
	wooden spoon
	mixing bowl

Chop the bacon and fry gently in the saucepan until crisp and brown. Add the chopped garlic and onion and the sliced mushrooms and cook until soft. Stir in the steak, tomato purée, salt and pepper to taste and sugar, and a little water if necessary. Bring to the boil.

Mix the flour, suet, parsley and a good pinch of salt in the bowl.

Add enough water to make a stiff dough, form into small balls and put on top of the meat mixture. Put on the lid, which should fit tightly, and simmer for 20 minutes without removing the lid. Serve with mashed potatoes and a green vegetable.

Sea pie

you will need	2 onions
	2 oz. mushrooms
	1 oz. dripping
	2 carrots
	1 lb. potatoes
	1 medium-sized can tomatoes
	1 1 lb. can braised steak
	salt and pepper
	2 pinches marjoram
	6 oz. self-raising flour
	3 oz. shredded suet
equipment	*knife and chopping board*
	large saucepan and lid
	potato peeler
	can opener
	mixing bowl
	tablespoon
	metal foil if saucepan
	lid is a poor fit

Chop the onions and mushrooms and fry until soft in the dripping. Peel and slice the carrots and peel and quarter the potatoes and add to the pan. Now mix in the tomatoes and if necessary add a little water. The potatoes should just be covered. Bring to the boil and cook for 10 minutes. Add the canned meat, stir again, season to taste and add the marjoram.

Mix together the flour, suet, $\frac{1}{2}$ teaspoon salt in the bowl and add enough water to make a stiff dough. Flour the dried chopping board and pat out the dough to a round that will exactly fit the saucepan. Bring the meat and vegetables to the boil, put the dough on top, replace the lid firmly and cook for 40 minutes without lifting the lid.

Jambalaya

you will need	1 chopped onion
	1 chopped clove garlic
	1 sweet green pepper
	2 oz. butter
	2 tablespoons olive oil
	¼ pint dry white wine
	1 large can Italian tomatoes
	pinch marjoram
	½ teaspoon crushed thyme
	salt and pepper
	few drops tabasco sauce
	8 oz. rice
	8 oz. canned ham, diced
	7 oz. can prawns
equipment	*knife and chopping board*
	large frying pan and lid
	can opener
	tablespoon
	teaspoon
	wooden spoon
	asbestos mat

Fry the onion and garlic with the de-seeded, sliced sweet pepper in the butter and olive oil. Add the wine, tomatoes, herbs, salt and pepper and a few drops of tabasco and bring to the boil.

Gradually stir in the rice, cover the pan and simmer very gently for about 20 minutes. Add the ham and prawns, mix well and continue to cook for another 10 minutes, or until the rice is tender.

Tastes marvellous out of doors.

Ham with rice

you will need	1 lb. canned ham, diced
	1 tablespoon olive oil
	1 oz. butter
	1 large onion, chopped
	1 clove garlic, chopped
	4 oz. mushrooms, sliced
	1 chicken stock cube
	$\frac{1}{4}$ pint dry white wine
	1 small can tomatoes
	marjoram and sage
	1 teaspoon sugar
	salt and pepper
	8 oz. rice
	Parmesan cheese
equipment	*knife and chopping board*
	frying pan and lid
	can opener
	large saucepan for rice
	tablespoon
	teaspoon
	wooden spoon
	jug or cup
	asbestos mat

Fry the ham in the oil and butter until golden brown. Remove from the pan and put in the onion and garlic, fry for a minute or two and add the mushrooms. Cook gently until they are soft, add the chicken cube dissolved in the wine, the canned tomatoes, a pinch of marjoram and a pinch of sage, sugar, salt and freshly ground black pepper to taste. Cover the pan and simmer gently for about 20 minutes, stirring occasionally. Replace the ham and heat through. If the sauce is too thick add a little water.

Serve with boiled rice, see page 110 and sprinkle with grated Parmesan cheese.

145

Neapolitan spaghetti

To serve 4

you will need	1 onion
	1 oz. butter
	1 teaspoon marjoram
	1 medium-sized can tomatoes
	1 teaspoon sugar
	bay leaf
	salt and pepper
	8 oz. spaghetti
	grated Parmesan cheese
equipment	*knife and chopping board*
	frying pan and lid
	teaspoon
	can opener
	wooden spoon
	large saucepan and lid
	strainer
	wooden spoon

Chop the onion finely and cook in the melted butter until soft.

Stir in the marjoram, tomatoes, sugar, bay leaf and salt and pepper to taste. Bring to the boil, cover the pan and simmer very gently for at least 20 minutes.

If the sauce is too thin cook uncovered for a few minutes until the consistency is right.

Cook the spaghetti in plenty of fast boiling salted water for about 12 minutes.

Drain well, pour the sauce over it and sprinkle with Parmesan cheese.

Shepherd's pie

you will need	1 large onion
	2 oz. mushrooms
	1 oz. olive oil or dripping
	1 large can minced beef
	1 large packet instant potato
	butter and milk
	salt and pepper
equipment	*tin or heatproof bowl*
	knife and chopping board
	frying pan
	can opener
	wooden spoon
	saucepan for potato
	salamander or metal sheet, optional

Fill the tin or heatproof bowl with very hot water.

Chop the onion and mushrooms and fry gently in the oil until soft. Stir in the minced beef, and taste before adding seasoning because some brands are rather highly spiced and seasoned. Prepare the instant potato according to the instructions on the packet.

When the meat mixture is really hot put it into the heated bowl and spread the potato over the top.

If you have a grill you can brown the top of the potatoes. If not, you may like to heat a salamander or metal sheet (this is very easy on an open fire) and carefully brown the top of your Shepherd's pie with this.

Spaghetti Bolognese

To serve 4

you will need	1 tablespoon oil
	1 oz. butter
	1 onion
	1 clove garlic
	1 large can minced beef
	2 oz. mushrooms
	4 tablespoons tomato purée
	wine or stock
	salt and pepper
	3 teaspoons sugar
	marjoram
	8 oz. spaghetti
	Parmesan cheese
equipment	*knife and chopping board*
	frying pan with lid
	large saucepan
	tablespoon
	teaspoon
	wooden spoon
	strainer for spaghetti
	can opener

Heat the oil and butter in a frying pan and fry the chopped onion and garlic until soft. Stir in the minced beef and the sliced mushrooms, the tomato purée and a little wine or stock. Cans of minced beef vary greatly in the amount of gravy they contain, and the amount of seasoning, so you will have to adjust these as necessary. Add what you need, plus the sugar and a little marjoram, cover the pan and simmer for at least 20 minutes. If you can manage to cook the sauce for longer the flavour will improve immeasurably, and if you *should* happen to have 1—2 chicken livers handy, these, finely chopped and added with the minced beef, will make it absolutely delicious.

Cook the spaghetti in plenty of fast boiling salted water,

until it is 'al dente'. About 12 minutes should be right, but test it in plenty of time as it really is rather nasty over-cooked. Drain it well, stir in some butter, and pour the hot sauce over it. Sprinkle with Parmesan cheese.

Mountain risotto

To serve 4

you will need	1 large onion
	1 oz. bacon fat
	6 oz. Patna rice
	2 tablespoons tomato purée
	¾ pint water
	1 bouillon cube
	1 teaspoon marjoram
	salt and pepper
	1 teaspoon sugar
	1 large can minced steak
	2 oz. grated cheese
equipment	*knife and chopping board*
	large frying pan and lid
	tablespoon
	teaspoon
	wooden spoon
	can opener
	asbestos mat

Chop the onion and fry in the bacon fat until soft. Stir in the rice and cook until transparent, then add the tomato purée, half the water, the bouillon cube, marjoram and salt and pepper and sugar to taste. Stir well, cover the pan and cook for 20 minutes, adding more water if necessary. Stir in the minced steak and cook for a further 10 minutes. The amount of liquid you need to add will depend on the gravy in the can — the risotto should be moist but not sloppy.

Serve when the rice is tender and sprinkle with grated cheese.

Corned beef hash

you will need	1 small onion
	2 oz. butter
	1 lb. cooked potatoes
	12 oz. can corned beef
	salt and pepper
	1 tablespoon evaporated milk
equipment	*knife and chopping board*
	large frying pan and lid
	can opener
	tablespoon
	fish slice
	asbestos mat

Chop the onion and fry it until brown in the butter. Roughly chop the potatoes and the corned beef and add to the pan. Season to taste, add the milk, stir it all up and leave on a very low heat until golden brown underneath. Try to serve it upside down, it looks better that way.

Corned beef paprika

To serve 4

you will need	1 lb. potatoes
	3 sticks celery
	1 large onion
	1 sweet pepper
	12 oz. can corned beef
	1 can tomatoes
	1 teaspoon paprika
	1 beef cube
	seasoning
equipment	*chopping board and knife*
	saucepan with lid

Put peeled and sliced potatoes into a saucepan with chopped

150

celery, chopped onion, and de-seeded and chopped pepper. Cook until tender (about 20 minutes) in approximately ½ pint of water. Take off the heat. Add the chopped up corned beef and the can of tomatoes. Crumble and dissolve the beef cube in a cupful of the stock, and pour it back into the saucepan. Season to taste. Cook for another 10 minutes so that tomatoes and corned beef are heated through. If sauce appears thin, thicken with a little cornflour.

Sausages in cider

To serve **4**

you will need	2 onions
	1 clove garlic, optional
	1 oz. butter
	1 large can pork sausages
	1 small can tomatoes
	1 dessertspoon flour
	¼ pint cider
	salt and pepper
equipment	*knife and chopping board*
	large frying pan and lid
	can opener
	dessertspoon
	wooden spoon
	cup and teaspoon

Fry the chopped onions and garlic in the butter for 2 or 3 minutes, then add the sausages and brown all over. Add the tomatoes and cook for a few moments, then blend the flour with the cider and add to the pan. Season to taste and bring to the boil, stirring. Cover the pan and cook for 20 minutes, stirring occasionally.

Serve with mashed potato, instant will do and a green vegetable.

Cheerful camp chilli

To serve 4

you will need
1 onion
1 oz. butter
1 large can minced beef
1 small can tomatoes
1 medium-sized can beans,
    haricot, broad or baked
salt and pepper
pinch chilli powder or few drops chilli sauce

equipment
knife and chopping board
large saucepan and lid
can opener
wooden spoon

This dish is very easy, very quick and very filling.

Chop the onion finely and fry it gently in the butter until soft. Then open all the cans and tip the contents into the pan. Stir it all up thoroughly, season to taste with salt and pepper and chilli powder or sauce. Don't forget that the chilli is very hot — add a little to start with and taste it.

Meat fritters

To serve 4 – 6

you will need
4 oz. flour
seasoning
1 egg
scant ½ pint milk and water
can of chopped pork
oil or fat to fry

equipment
bowl and fork
frying pan

Sieve flour and seasoning, add the egg, gradually beat in the liquid. Continue beating until smooth and leave standing for as long as possible. Cut the meat into slices. Heat the fat. Coat the slices of meat with the batter, and fry in the hot fat. Serve with rings of apple pineapple or vegetables.

Sweet and sour sausages

To serve 4

you will need	1 large can pork sausages
	1 oz. frying fat
	1 large onion
	1 sweet green pepper
	1 oz. flour
	1 medium-sized can pineapple pieces
	2 tablespoons brown sugar or honey
	2 tablespoons vinegar
	salt and pepper
	8 oz. Patna rice
equipment	*can opener*
	large frying pan with lid
	chopping board and knife
	saucepan for rice
	tablespoons
	wooden spoon
	asbestos mat

Fry the sausages in the fat until nicely brown. Remove them from the pan and fry the chopped onion and the de-seeded, sliced green pepper. When they are soft, stir in the flour and then add the juice from the canned pineapple and a little water. Bring slowly to the boil, stirring all the time, and then add all the other ingredients including the sausages, and season to taste. Simmer very gently for $\frac{1}{2}$ hour and if the sauce gets too thick add a little more water.

Serve with fluffy boiled rice, see page 110.

Casserole of frankfurters

To serve 4

you will need	2 onions
	1 clove garlic
	1 oz. butter
	6 oz. rice
	1 small can tomatoes
	$\frac{1}{2}$ pint stock
	1 teaspoon sugar
	salt and pepper
	few drops tabasco sauce
	$4\frac{1}{2}$ oz. packet frozen peas
	1 large can frankfurters
equipment	*sharp knife and board*
	large frying pan with lid
	tablespoon, teaspoon
	wooden spoon
	jug if bouillon cube is used for stock
	can opener

Fry chopped onions and garlic in butter until soft. Stir in the rice and cook for a few minutes, then add the tomatoes and the stock. Stir in the sugar and the salt and pepper to taste.

The amount of tabasco you use is a matter of taste, but it's very hot, so start with a very little and keep tasting until it's right.

Cook, covered, for about 20 minutes, stirring now and then and adding more liquid if necessary. When the rice is cooked stir in the frozen peas and sliced frankfurters and heat through.

If liked, sprinkle over a little grated Parmesan cheese.

154

Frankfurters in mushroom and onion sauce

To serve 4

you will need
1 large can frankfurters
1 oz. butter
1 oz. flour
4 oz. mushrooms
2 onions
$\frac{1}{2}$ pint milk
salt and pepper

equipment
can opener
saucepan and lid
knife and chopping board
small pan for sauce
wooden spoon
jug and fork if using
dried milk

Put the frankfurters into the saucepan with water to cover and bring to the boil.

Put the lid on and stand them on the grass or somewhere out of the way. Heat the butter for the sauce, stir in the flour after you have softened the chopped mushrooms and onions.

Add the milk which can be fresh, evaporated, or reconstituted dried milk, stirring all the time. Season to taste with salt and freshly ground black pepper. Drain the frankfurters, dish them up and pour the sauce over them.

Good with mashed potato, instant potato will do, and a green vegetable.

Barbecued frankfurters

To serve 4

you will need	1 medium-sized onion
	2 tablespoons butter
	2 tablespoons vinegar
	2 tablespoons brown sugar
	4 tablespoons lemon juice
	1 tablespoon Worcestershire sauce
	$\frac{1}{2}$ tablespoon made mustard
	1 stick celery
	2 tablespoons water
	salt and pepper
	1 large can frankfurters
equipment	*saucepan and lid*
	knife and chopping board
	tablespoon
	teaspoon
	wooden spoon
	fork
	can opener

Brown onion in the butter, add the rest of the ingredients except the frankfurters, and cook slowly for about 20 minutes, stirring occasionally. Prick the skins of the frankfurters, add to the sauce until they are heated right through.

Good with potato croquettes, (see page 179 omitting the cheese), if you don't mind rather a lot of washing up. Or, serve with a potato salad, see page 63.

Frankfurters in curry sauce

To serve 4

you will need	1 carrot
	1 onion
	1 clove garlic
	1 oz. dripping
	1 small can tomatoes
	$\frac{1}{4}$ pint red wine
	1 teaspoon sugar
	salt and pepper
	1 tablespoon curry powder
	1 large can frankfurters
equipment	*knife and board*
	frying pan and lid
	wooden spoon
	teaspoon
	tablespoon
	can opener
	saucepan and lid

Chop the carrot, onion and garlic and fry in the dripping until soft. Add the tomatoes, wine, sugar, salt and pepper to taste and the curry powder. Simmer for about 20 minutes.

10 minutes before the sauce is ready, cover the frankfurters with water, bring to the boil, remove from the heat and allow to stand.

Serve with boiled rice, see page 110.

Variation:

Sliced spam or luncheon meat can be used in place of frankfurters, in which case the meat should be heated gently through in the sauce.

Crab and cucumber

To serve 4

you will need
4 oz. grated cheese
½ pint Béchamel sauce, see page 185
1 large can crab
6 oz. rice
½ cucumber
paprika

equipment
small saucepan
serving dish
large pan and lid
grater or potato peeler
knife
can opener

Add the grated cheese to the Béchamel sauce and stir until melted. Separate the crab into pieces and stir this in as well. Heat for about 5 minutes but do not allow to boil. Pour over the cooked rice, see page 110, garnish with very thin slices of cucumber and dust with paprika.

Fish and potato cakes

To serve 4

you will need
small can pink salmon
½ lb. mashed potatoes
egg to bind
seasoning
flour
oil or fat to fry

equipment
can opener
fork and bowl
frying pan

Break up salmon, remove bones. Mix well with potato, seasoning and egg. Shape into flat cakes using floury hands. Fry in hot fat.

Fish risotto

you will need	1 sweet green pepper
	2 onions
	1 tablespoon oil
	1 oz. butter
	6 oz. rice
	1 large can tuna or salmon
	1 small can prawns
	1 small can tomatoes
	1 teaspoon sugar
	salt and pepper
	lemon juice
	chopped parsley
equipment	*sharp knife*
	chopping board
	large frying pan and lid
	can opener
	wooden spoon
	tablespoon
	teaspoon

De-seed the pepper and chop it with the onions. Fry them gently in the oil and butter until soft, then stir in the rice and cook until it is transparent. Open the cans of fish halfway and pour the liquid from each into the frying pan, stir in the tomatoes and the sugar and salt and pepper to taste. Cover the pan and simmer gently for about 20 minutes, stirring occasionally, until the rice is cooked. It may be necessary to add a little more liquid. When the rice is cooked, add a squeeze of lemon juice and the fish, and heat for another 3 minutes.

Sprinkle with chopped parsley and serve with a green salad.

Chinese fried rice with prawns

To serve 4

you will need	2 tablespoons olive oil
	1 large onion
	1 sweet green pepper
	6 oz. boiled rice, see page 110
	1 large can prawns or shrimps
	2 tablespoons soy sauce
	salt and pepper
	2 eggs
equipment	*large frying pan*
	knife and chopping board
	can opener
	tablespoon
	fork and small jug
	wooden spoon

Heat the oil in the frying pan and cook the chopped onion and the de-seeded, chopped sweet pepper until soft. Stir in the cooked rice, raise the heat and cook, stirring, until the rice begins to turn brown.

Add the prawns and the soy sauce, and a little salt and pepper to taste. The soy sauce is already quite salty. When the mixture is heated through stir in the beaten eggs and cook for another 2 minutes.

Variation

A can of crab meat can be used instead of the prawns.

Egg and prawn curry

you will need	1 small onion
	2 oz. butter
	1 tablespoon curry powder
	1 level tablespoon flour
	1 tablespoon tomato purée
	½ pint water
	1 teaspoon sugar
	lemon juice
	salt and pepper
	6 oz. can prawns
	8 oz. long grain rice
	8 hard-boiled eggs
equipment	*knife and chopping board*
	frying pan and lid
	tablespoon
	wooden spoon
	can opener
	saucepan and lid for rice

Fry the chopped onion gently in the butter until soft. Add the curry powder to the pan, stir well and cook for a few more minutes. Stir in the flour, then add the tomato purée, water, sugar, lemon juice and salt and pepper to taste, stirring all the time and bringing slowly to the boil. Simmer for 5 minutes, then add the prawns and heat through, adjust the seasoning and add more curry powder if required.

Slice the hard-boiled eggs lengthways and arrange them on the cooked rice, see page 110. Pour the sauce over the eggs and serve with 1 or more of the side dishes, see page 165.

Jiffy Mexicana

To serve 4

you will need	2 oz. butter
	1 onion
	2 dessertspoons curry powder
	small can tomatoes
	little water
	1 tablespoon seeded raisins
	1 large can tuna
	salt and pepper
	1 lemon
equipment	*chopping board and knife*
	can opener
	saucepan

Melt the butter in a saucepan, and lightly fry chopped onion until transparent; do not brown. Add the curry powder and allow to cook 2 minutes, stirring. Pour in the canned tomatoes and a little water to thin. Add the raisins, and the broken up tuna. Season. Bring to boil, and cook on gentle heat for 10—15 minutes. Then add the juice of half a lemon and the grated zest of a lemon.

Serve with boiled rice, see page 110.

Variations

A sweet pepper is optional, but tastes good in this curry. It should be de-seeded and chopped and fried lightly with the onion.

Fresh tomatoes can be used instead of canned ones. Use 4—6 tomatoes and $\frac{1}{4}$ pint water.

If you like garlic, add a crushed clove, with the onion.

Prawn-stuffed green peppers

To serve 4

you will need	4 large green peppers
	3 cloves garlic
	1 oz. butter
	$\frac{1}{4}$ teaspoon ginger
	$\frac{1}{4}$ teaspoon chilli
	$\frac{1}{2}$ teaspoon paprika
	1 teaspoon salt
	$\frac{1}{2}$ teaspoon cummin
	$\frac{1}{4}$ teaspoon turmeric
	6 oz. can prawns
	6 onions
	tomato sauce, see page 186
equipment	*chopping board and knife*
	saucepan with lid
	small saucepan

Cut off tops of green peppers and take out the seeds. Scald in hot water and set aside. Chop the garlic very fine. Heat the butter in a frying pan and fry the garlic, ginger, chilli, paprika, salt, cummin and turmeric for 5 minutes. Then add the broken up prawns and well-chopped onions, stirring the mixture now and again so that it does not burn. Turn the flame low and cover pan. Simmer until prawns are soft. Stuff the mixture into the prepared green peppers. Put on 'lids' of peppers and stand them up in a tomato sauce, in a saucepan, if possible, one in which they can be wedged side-by-side. Make sauce as recipe on page 186, but making the liquid of tomatoes up to $\frac{1}{2}$ pint with water. Fit lid on saucepan and cook peppers in tomato sauce over a low heat for 30 minutes, or until flesh is tender. Serve with boiled or fried rice, see pages 110 and 37.

New Zealand curry

you will need	2 onions
	1 oz. dripping or lard
	1 cooking apple
	1 carrot
	1 tablespoon chutney
	1 tablespoon curry powder
	pinch ginger
	1 tablespoon coconut
	1 large can minced beef
	2 oz. cashew nuts
	salt and pepper
equipment	*knife and chopping board*
	large frying pan and lid
	tablespoon
	wooden spoon
	can opener

Fry the sliced onions in the dripping or lard until soft. Chop the peeled apple and carrot, add to the pan and fry for a few more minutes.

Stir in the chutney and curry powder, more than 1 tablespoon of curry powder if liked; add the ginger, coconut, the minced beef and the nuts and cook, covered, for about 15 minutes.

Adjust the seasoning, and if the mixture is too thick stir in a little milk.

Serve with boiled rice, see page 110 and several side dishes, see page 165.

Note

Almost anything can be used in place of the minced beef: cold diced meat, lobster, chicken, hard-boiled eggs.

New Delhi curried beef

To serve 4

you will need	2 onions
	2 oz. dripping
	2 cooking apples
	1 large can minced beef
	1 tablespoon curry powder
	salt and pepper
	1 tablespoon coconut
equipment	*knife and chopping board*
	frying pan and lid
	potato peeler
	can opener
	tablespoon
	wooden spoon

Fry the sliced onions in the dripping until golden brown, then add the peeled and diced apples. Stir in the minced beef and the curry powder, and season to taste. Simmer for about 20 minutes, stirring occasionally, sprinkle with coconut, and serve with fluffy boiled rice, see page 110.

Serve with side dishes, see below.

Suggestions for side dishes to serve with curry:

mango chutney	tomatoes
ginger	chopped hard-boiled egg
pine nuts	chopped sweet peppers
pistachio nuts	orange
almonds	banana
cashews	apple
coconut	pineapple
raisins	peach halves with cream cheese
onion rings	prunes stuffed with cottage cheese
chopped ham	any fruit chutney
cucumber in yoghourt	any combination of the above

Vegetables

Fortunately the high season for sailing and camping is also the time of vegetable plenty. And on the Continent where food prices are generally high it is pleasant to find the abundant vegetables on their colourful stalls relatively cheap.

In this country no one has a better chance of buying dew fresh produce than the sailor or camper. Cottage gardeners frequently produce more than they need, and are pleased to sell them, and many lock keepers on our waterways also run a small market garden and will pick crisp tender beans for you while you wait.

Treat this perfect produce as it deserves in the same way as the French do — serve it as a course on its own. Either dress it simply with butter and a little freshly ground black pepper, or cook two or more vegetables together for exciting combinations of flavour — and less washing up.

Fried aubergine

To serve 4

you will need	1 large aubergine
	1 teaspoon salt
	1 egg
	flour for coating
	2 tablespoons olive oil
equipment	*knife*
	frying pan
	dish and plate
	heavy weight
	small bowl and fork
	tablespoon

Wash the aubergine, peel and cut into ¾-inch slices. Add salt. Put them in the dish with the plate over them and the weight on top and leave for 30 minutes. Pour off the liquid, dip each slice in beaten egg and then flour, and fry in the oil over moderate heat until brown on both sides.

Red cabbage with apple

To serve 4

you will need	1 large cooking apple
	1 small red cabbage
	1 large onion
	1 dessertspoon sugar
	1 oz. butter
	salt and pepper
	1 tablespoon wine vinegar
equipment	*knife and board*
	saucepan with lid
	dessertspoon
	tablespoon
	wooden spoon
	asbestos mat

Slice the apple, onion and cabbage fairly finely, removing the stalk from the cabbage. Put all the ingredients together in the pan and cook over a very gentle heat for about 1 hour, stirring occasionally.

Globe artichokes

To serve 4

you will need	4 small artichokes
	salt
	melted butter
equipment	*sharp knife*
	saucepan and lid

Artichokes should have green, supple leaves — if the tips of the leaves are turning brown don't buy them, they have had their day. Cut off the stalks and remove the tough outer leaves, then wash in several changes of water to remove any insects. Drain well. Cook in plenty of boiling salted water for 30 minutes, or until tender, but don't over do it or they will become tasteless. They are cooked when the leaves pull out easily.

When tender, drain upside down, then remove the choke — the small fluffy leaves in the centre. Serve with lots of melted butter.

Corn fritters

To serve 4

you will need	1 small can sweet corn
	4 oz. self-raising flour
	½ teaspoon salt
	½ teaspoon paprika
	1 egg
	fat for frying
equipment	*can opener*
	bowl and fork
	teaspoon
	jug and whisk
	saucepan
	perforated spoon

Drain the sweet corn and mash it. Add the flour, salt and paprika and mix well. Separate the egg, mix the yolk into the sweetcorn mixture, beat the white until stiff and then fold in. Fry in spoonfuls in hot fat until golden brown. Do not overcook. Good with bacon.

French beans with garlic

you will need	2 cloves garlic
	2 lb. small crisp French beans
	salt and pepper
	2 oz. butter
	chopped parsley
equipment	*knife and board*
	large saucepan and lid

Chop the garlic finely and put into the pan with water and salt to taste.

Bring to the boil and cook the beans until just tender, then drain well, add the butter and freshly ground black pepper and sprinkle with chopped parsley.

Do as the French do and eat them as a separate course.

Cucumber with lemons

To serve 4

you will need	1 good cucumber
	salt
	2 oz. butter
	juice 1 lemon
equipment	*sharp knife*
	saucepan and lid
	small bowl or cup
	lemon squeezer

Peel and dice the cucumber and boil it in salted water for 8 minutes. In the meantime mix the butter with as much of the lemon juice as it will take. Drain the cucumber and top with the butter, stirring it in as it melts.

Carrots and onions

you will need	2 oz. butter
	2 large onions
	3 lb. new carrots
	salt and pepper
	1 teaspoon sugar
equipment	*knife and chopping board*
	frying pan or saucepan
	wooden spoon
	teaspoon

Heat the butter in the pan and fry the chopped onions gently until soft.

Stir in the peeled and sliced carrots and the sugar and season to taste. Barely cover with water, put the lid on and cook gently until the carrots are tender.

Carrots Vichy

you will need	1 lb. young carrots
	salt
	1 oz. butter
	1 teaspoon sugar
	chopped parsley
equipment	*sharp knife*
	board
	saucepan and lid
	teaspoon

Scrape and slice the carrots and cook for 10 minutes in boiling, salted water. Pour off the water, add the butter and sugar to the pan and cook for another 5 minutes. Serve sprinkled with chopped parsley.

Courgettes aux tomates

To serve 4

you will need	1 lb. courgettes
	salt, pepper
	2 tomatoes
	2 oz. butter .
equipment	*knife and chopping board*
	dish
	jug or bowl
	frying pan

Peel the courgettes and slice them. Put them in the dish, cover with salt and leave for 30 minutes. Pour boiling water over the tomatoes, leave for 5 minutes then peel and slice them. Drain the courgettes and fry them in the butter with the sliced tomatoes. Add salt and pepper to taste.

Leeks Lucullus

To serve 4

you will need	1 lb. potatoes
	2 lb. leeks
	2 oz. grated cheese
	salt and pepper
	1 oz. butter
	little evaporated milk
equipment	*knife and chopping board*
	large saucepan and lid
	tin or heatproof serving dish
	fork

Peel the potatoes and cut them fairly small, and wash and slice the leeks. Boil them together in salted water for about twenty minutes. Meanwhile, pour very hot water into your serving dish and leave to stand. Mash the potatoes and leeks when they are cooked, with half the cheese, pepper, butter, and evaporated milk, until smooth and creamy. Turn them into your heatproof dish, sprinkle more grated cheese on top and brown them under the grill.

Leeks and tomatoes To serve 4

you will need	1½ lb. leeks
	1 oz. butter
	3 tomatoes
	salt and pepper
	½ teaspoon sugar
equipment	*sharp knife and board*
	saucepan and lid
	teaspoon

Wash the leeks very thoroughly. Cut away the root and most of the green, then slice into 1-inch pieces. Fry in the butter in the covered pan until soft but do not allow to brown. Add the chopped, peeled tomatoes, salt and pepper to taste, and the sugar, and cook for another 5 minutes with the lid off.

Variation

If you have a grill, you can pour cooked leeks and tomatoes mixture into a shallow dish, top it with a mixture of 2 oz. grated Cheddar cheese and 2 − 3 oz. breadcrumbs, and put it under the grill for 5 − 10 minutes to crisp.

Petits pois à la flamande

To serve 4

you will need	1½ lb. young green peas
	1 bunch baby carrots
	1 teaspoon sugar
	2 oz. butter
	salt and pepper
	1 small bunch parsley
equipment	*sharp knife*
	saucepan and lid

Shell the peas and scrape the carrots and leave them whole.
Put the carrots in the saucepan with the sugar, butter, and
salt and pepper to taste. Add enough water to cover. Boil
fairly fast for about 10 minutes. Now add the shelled peas
and the parsley and continue to cook quite fast until the
carrots are tender and the water has disappeared. Remove
the parsley before serving.

Sweet peppers with tomato and corn

To serve 4

you will need	2 firm tomatoes
	1 large packet frozen sweet corn
	2 sweet green peppers
	salt and pepper
	2 oz. butter
equipment	*knife and board*
	saucepan and lid
	small bowl

Put ½ pint of water into saucepan and bring to the boil.
Make a cross with the point of a knife in the stalk end of the

174

tomatoes and put in the bowl. Pour a little of the boiling water on to them.

Add the sweet corn to the rest of the water in the saucepan, bring to the boil again and cook for 3 minutes. Remove the seeds from the sweet peppers, cut into thin rings, and peel and slice the tomatoes. Add to the sweet corn, cook for 2 minutes, drain, season to taste and dot with butter before serving.

Finnish mushrooms with sour cream

To serve 4

you will need	2 oz. butter
	1 small onion
	12 oz. sliced mushrooms
	salt and pepper
	good pinch nutmeg
	$\frac{1}{4}$ pint sour cream
equipment	*knife and chopping board*
	saucepan and lid
	wooden spoon

Melt the butter in the pan and cook the chopped onion until soft.

Add the mushrooms, salt and freshly ground black pepper and nutmeg to taste. Cook over a medium heat, stirring occasionally, until the mushrooms are browned. Remove from the stove and heat through again after adding the sour cream.

Good on toast with crisp grilled bacon.

Pepperoni

To serve 4

you will need	1 large onion
	1 clove garlic
	1 oz. butter
	2 sweet green peppers
	2 sweet red peppers
	salt and pepper
equipment	*knife and chopping board*
	large frying pan and lid

Slice the onion and chop the garlic finely. Cook slowly in the butter until soft, then add the de-seeded and sliced peppers and season to taste. Cook all together until just tender.

Ratatouille

To serve 4

you will need	2 large onions
	2 sweet green peppers
	2 aubergines
	4 tomatoes
	3 tablespoons oil
	salt and pepper
equipment	*knife and chopping board*
	tablespoon
	saucepan or frying pan with lid

Slice the onions, de-seed the peppers and slice them, slice the unpeeled aubergines and peel and chop the tomatoes. Fry them all in the oil very gently, starting with the onions and when they are soft adding the aubergines and sweet peppers. After about 25 minutes add the tomatoes, and cook for another 10 minutes, without a lid if this is possible. Season to taste.

This is a Provençal dish and should really be made with a great deal more olive oil, but this amount is probably quite enough for English tastes.

Pommes de terre en matelote

To serve 4

you will need	1½ lb. potatoes
	salt
	2 tablespoons wine
	2 oz. butter
	1 tablespoon chopped chives
	pepper
	1 yolk egg
	1 tablespoon chopped parsley
equipment	*knife and chopping board*
	saucepan and lid
	tablespoon
	potato peeler
	cup and fork

Peel the potatoes and cut them into pieces half the size of an egg. Boil in just enough salted water to cover. When they are tender but only just so, pour away ½ the water and add the wine, butter, chives and plenty of freshly ground black pepper. Cook gently for 5 minutes, then stir in the beaten egg yolk, being careful not to break up the potatoes. Sprinkle with chopped parsley before serving.

You could use the egg white for Cream whip, see page 199.

Sauté potatoes

you will need	1½ lb. potatoes
	salt
	fairly deep fat or
	oil for frying
equipment	*sharp knife*
	saucepan and lid
	pan for frying
	potato peeler
	perforated spoon

Boil the peeled potatoes in salted water for 10 minutes. Cut into pieces half the size of an egg and drop into the hot fat. Cook until golden brown.

Paprika potatoes

To serve 4

you will need	2 tablespoons oil
	1 large onion
	2 level tablespoons flour
	2 teaspoons paprika
	¼ pint vinegar
	½ pint stock
	1½ lb. potatoes
	salt
equipment	*knife and chopping board*
	saucepan and lid
	tablespoon
	teaspoon
	potato peeler
	wooden spoon

Heat the oil in the saucepan and fry the chopped onion until soft. Stir in the flour and paprika, then add the vinegar

178

and stock gradually, stirring all the time, and bring to the boil.

Add the peeled potatoes cut to the size of half an egg and salt to taste.

Cover the pan and cook gently, stirring occasionally, until the potatoes are tender.

Delicious with sausages or cold meat.

Potato croquettes

you will need	3½ oz. packet instant potato
	1 egg yolk
	salt and pepper
	2 oz. finely grated cheese, optional
	1 egg
	breadcrumbs
	fairly deep fat for frying
equipment	*saucepan*
	fork
	grater
	cup for beaten egg
	plate for breadcrumbs
	perforated spoon
	kitchen paper

Prepare the potatoes according to the directions on the packet, but omitting the butter.

Stir in the egg yolk and season to taste. Add the cheese, if used.

Allow the mixture to get quite cold and then form into balls.

Coat with egg and breadcrumbs, flatten, and fry in the hot fat until golden brown.

Drain on kitchen paper before serving.

Potatoes Lyonnaise

To serve 4

you will need	1 lb. potatoes
	2 onions
	lard or dripping
	salt and pepper
	chopped parsley
equipment	*potato peeler*
	saucepan and lid
	knife and board
	frying pan

Peel and halve the potatoes and boil them in salted water for 10 minutes. Chop the onions finely and fry in hot lard or dripping for 2 minutes, then add the parboiled sliced potatoes, season to taste and cook until soft and light golden brown. Sprinkle with chopped parsley and serve.

Tomates provençales

To serve 4

you will need	4 large tomatoes
	1 clove garlic
	salt and pepper
	chopped parsley
	olive oil
equipment	*sharp knife*
	grill pan

Cut the tomatoes in 2, make a cross on the cut surface and rub with the cut clove of garlic. Season liberally with salt and freshly ground black pepper, press plenty of chopped parsley on to each tomato, sprinkle with olive oil and grill until very slightly blackened.

Beans with carrots and celery

To serve 4

you will need	small bunch carrots
	2 sticks celery
	1 pint stock
	salt
	freshly ground black pepper
	1 lb. runner beans
	1 oz. butter
equipment	*chopping board*
	sharp knife
	large saucepan with lid

Simmer the sliced carrots and chopped celery in the stock, with seasoning to taste, for about ten minutes. Then add the prepared beans with the butter and simmer until they are tender.

Chop-suey cabbage

To serve 4

you will need	1 onion
	1 oz. butter
	2 lb. firm cabbage
	3 – 4 tomatoes
	seasoning
equipment	*chopping board and knife*
	saucepan with lid

Chop up onion and fry lightly in the butter in a saucepan. Add the finely chopped cabbage, sliced tomatoes, and about 2 tablespoons water. Season well. Put on lid and cook for about 10 minutes, stirring from time to time. Try it with 2 oz. chopped up bacon cooked in half the fat with the onion.

181

Dahl

you will need	2 onions
	1 clove garlic
	2 tablespoons oil
	4 carrots
	½ lb. lentils
	1 tablespoon curry powder
	salt
	brown sugar
	2 tablespoons tomato purée
	½ pint stock
	lemon juice
equipment	*chopping board*
	sharp knife
	large saucepan and lid
	wooden spoon
	tablespoon
	lemon squeezer

Fry the chopped onions and garlic in the oil until they are golden brown. Add the carrots and lentils and stir well, then add the curry powder and cook over a very gentle heat for a few minutes, stirring all the time. Add the salt, sugar, tomato purée and stock and stir until boiling. Lower the heat and simmer gently for about 45 minutes or until the lentils are cooked. Add a little lemon juice, adjust the seasoning, and serve.

This is a vegetarian dish, very cheap and nutritious. If you are cooking in a country where meat is very expensive you may feel inclined to turn vegetarian for a day or two towards the end of the holiday.

Hungarian marrow

you will need	young 12-inch marrow
	4 oz. butter
	3 onions
	1 teaspoon paprika
	$\frac{1}{2}$ pint sour cream
	1 dessertspoon parsley
	salt and pepper
equipment	*chopping board and knife*
	saucepan with lid
	bowl

Scrape outside skin of marrow and wipe it. Cut it up into finger-sized strips without peeling it. If it is a young marrow, seeds should not be coarse, and should not need to be removed. Melt the butter in the saucepan. Peel and chop up the onions as small as possible and fry them light brown in the butter. Now add the marrow pieces. Cover the pan. Lower the heat to simmering point and cook for 15 minutes. Stir the paprika into the sour cream and mix well. Pour this over the marrow. Let it heat thoroughly. Chop the parsley and sprinkle over the marrow. It is now ready to serve.

Sauces

Sauces can transform plain meals into perfect ones.

In this section there are sauces for serving with the canned meats which are so useful to sailors and campers. There are also sauces for marinating, for basting meat over an open fire or a charcoal grill, or for both.

And then there are the sweet sauces for serving with puddings or with bought ice cream.

Béchamel sauce

you will need	½ pint milk
	1 slice onion
	few peppercorns
	1 bay leaf
	¾ oz. butter
	¾ oz. flour
	salt and pepper
equipment	*saucepan*
	asbestos mat
	knife
	jug
	wooden spoon

Put the milk, onion, peppercorns and bay leaf into the saucepan and heat very gently for about 5 minutes. The milk must not boil. Strain the milk into a jug. Wash the pan, heat the butter until melted and stir in the flour. Now add the milk away from the heat, a third at a time, stirring to keep the sauce smooth. Boil for 1 minute and season to taste.

Béchamel sauce is of coating consistency, and if a pouring sauce is required more liquid can be added.

Sauce mornay

you will need   Béchamel sauce, see page 185
                          3 oz. grated cheese
equipment   *grater or potato peeler*

Make the Béchamel with ½ pint milk and add the grated cheese stirring over a gentle heat until the cheese has melted and the sauce is smooth.

Tomato sauce

you will need   1 small can tomatoes
                          1 small onion
                          1 teaspoon sugar
                          salt and pepper
                          marjoram
                          1 dessertspoon flour
equipment   *knife and chopping board*
                          saucepan and lid
                          teaspoon
                          dessertspoon
                          wooden spoon
                          can opener
                          asbestos mat

Cook the tomatoes, chopped onion, sugar and salt and pepper and marjoram to taste for about 20 minutes, stirring from time to time and keeping the heat very low. I don't bother to sieve this when we're afloat or camping, but I will if anyone ever invents a disposable strainer.

Stir in the flour mixed with a little water to thicken it a little. Even with the pips it tastes good.

Paprika sauce

you will need
2 large onions
1½ oz. dripping
1½ oz. flour
2 teaspoons paprika
1 pint stock
2 tablespoons vinegar
salt

equipment
knife and chopping board
saucepan
tablespoon
teaspoon
wooden spoon

Fry the chopped onions in the dripping until soft, then stir in the flour and the paprika. Gradually add the stock, stirring well all the time, then the vinegar, and add salt to taste. Bring to the boil, stirring.

Very good with cold meat, particularly canned meat, fish and sausages.

Oxford sauce

you will need
2 tablespoons brown sugar
2 teaspoons made mustard
salt and pepper
6 tablespoons olive oil
2 tablespoons wine vinegar

equipment
jug or bowl
teaspoon
tablespoon
wooden spoon

Mix together the brown sugar and the mustard, add salt and pepper to taste, then gradually stir in the olive oil. Finally add the wine vinegar.

Spanish sauce

you will need	1 small sweet green pepper
	1 onion
	2 sticks celery
	1 small can tomatoes
	salt and pepper
	1 tablespoon flour
equipment	*knife and board*
	can opener
	saucepan and lid
	tablespoon
	cup and teaspoon

De-seed the pepper, and chop with the onion and celery. Put all these with the tomatoes into the saucepan, season to taste, bring to boiling point and simmer for about 20 minutes. Stir occasionally. Mix the flour with a little water, add to the brew and bring to the boil, stirring all the time.

Useful with cold meat and vegetables.

Cold cucumber sauce

you will need	$\frac{1}{2}$ large cucumber
	1 tablespoon wine vinegar
	salt and pepper
	2 tablespoons thick cream
equipment	*sharp knife and board*
	tablespoon
	small bowl or jug

Peel the cucumber and chop finely. Add the vinegar and salt and pepper to taste to the cream, and mix well. Drain the cucumber and mix into the cream.

Alternatively yoghourt may be used instead of the cream and vinegar.

188

Sweet-sour onion sauce

you will need
2 large onions
1½ oz. dripping
1½ oz. flour
1 pint stock
1 tablespoon brown sugar
2 tablespoons vinegar
salt and pepper

equipment
knife and chopping board
saucepan
tablespoon
wooden spoon

Fry the chopped onions in the dripping until soft. Stir in the flour then add the stock gradually, stirring all the time, and bring to the boil. Stir in the brown sugar and vinegar, season to taste, and serve with rissoles, corned beef hash, see page 150, fish or cold meat.

French dressing

you will need
1 tablespoon wine vinegar
½ level teaspoon dry mustard
1 level teaspoon salt
1 level teaspoon castor sugar
3 tablespoons olive oil
black pepper

equipment
bowl or jug
teaspoon
tablespoon
fork

Put all the ingredients into the bowl and whisk with the fork. When it has thickened a little adjust seasoning as necessary.

189

Vinaigrette dressing

To the French dressing, see page 189 add 1 tablespoon chopped thyme, parsley and chives, mixed.

Quick salad dressing

you will need	½ teaspoon dry mustard
	4 tablespoons olive oil
	juice ½ lemon
	½ teaspoon salt
	pepper
	¼ pint evaporated milk
equipment	*airtight plastic beaker with lid*
	tablespoon
	knife
	lemon squeezer
	teaspoon

Mix the mustard with the oil and lemon juice, add all the other ingredients, put on the lid and shake vigorously until well mixed and smooth.

Yoghourt salad dressing

you will need	1 carton unflavoured yoghourt
	1 tablespoon lemon juice or vinegar
	1 teaspoon sugar
equipment	*jug*
	tablespoon
	teaspoon

Stir all the ingredients vigorously together.

Cheese dressing for lettuce

you will need
2 oz. blue cheese
1 tablespoon wine vinegar
2 tablespoons olive oil
salt and pepper to taste

equipment
small bowl or jug
tablespoon
fork

Place everything together in the bowl and whisk together with the fork.

Red mustard sauce

you will need
$\frac{1}{2}$ small onion
2 oz. butter
2 teaspoons dry mustard
4 teaspoons water
3 tablespoons red currant jelly

equipment
knife and chopping board
teaspoon
tablespoon
wooden spoon
cup

Chop the onion very finely and fry gently in the butter until soft. Remove from the heat. Mix the mustard with the water and stir into the onion with the jelly. Serve hot or cold with tinned meat, sausages, lamb or pork kebabs, pressed beef, etc. Bramble or elderberry jelly will do equally well.

Easy basting sauce

you will need	3 tablespoons wine vinegar
	3 tablespoons fresh lemon juice
	4 tablespoons olive oil
	$\frac{1}{2}$ teaspoon soy sauce
	freshly ground black pepper
	salt
equipment	*bowl*
	for or whisk

Put liquid ingredients together in a bowl. Add salt and freshly ground black pepper to taste.

This sauce can be used to baste steaks, chops, poultry etc. as it is grilled or barbecued.

Barbecue sauce 1

you will need	1 oz. butter
	1 clove garlic
	$\frac{1}{2}$ small onion
	$\frac{1}{2}$ sweet green pepper
	2 teaspoons cornflour
	1 tablespoon tomato purée
	3 oz. soft brown sugar
	1 tablespoon wine vinegar
	salt and pepper
	$\frac{1}{2}$ teaspoon tabasco sauce
	$\frac{1}{4}$ pint water
equipment	*knife and chopping board*
	small pan
	teaspoon
	tablespoon
	wooden spoon

Melt the butter in the pan and fry the chopped garlic and

onion for 2 minutes. Remove the seeds from the sweet pepper and shred finely and add to the pan. Cook gently until soft. Stir in the cornflour and all the other ingredients and bring to the boil, stirring all the time.

Serve with cold meats, kebabs, sausages, frankfurters or fish.

Barbecue sauce 2

you will need	1 oz. oil or butter
	2 teaspoons flour
	1 small can tomatoes
	1 teaspoon sugar
	salt and pepper
	$\frac{1}{4}$ pint stock or water potatoes have been cooked in
	1 tablespoon soy sauce
	1 teaspoon Worcestershire sauce
equipment	*saucepan*
	teaspoon
	can opener
	wooden spoon
	tablespoon

Melt the oil or butter and stir in the flour. Add the tomatoes, sugar, salt and pepper to taste, stock and sauces, and bring to tne boil, stirring all the time. Lower the heat and simmer for at least 10 minutes.

Lemon barbecue sauce

you will need
1 small onion
juice 2 lemons
$\frac{1}{4}$ pint olive oil
3 teaspoons chopped herbs
salt and pepper
few drops tabasco

equipment
knife and chopping board
large bowl or pan
lemon squeezer
teaspoon

Chop the onion finely and mix with all the other ingredients. This sauce is good as a marinade for chicken but don't use too much tabasco or it will swamp the taste of the chicken.

Mint and onion sauce for lamb

you will need
several sprigs of mint
1 small onion
$\frac{1}{4}$ pint oil
$\frac{1}{4}$ pint red wine
salt and pepper
good pinch sugar

equipment
shallow bowl and spoon
knife and chopping board
measuring jug

Bruise the mint well and put with the chopped onion into the bowl. Pour on the oil and wine and season to taste with salt, pepper and sugar. The cubed lamb can be marinated overnight, and then basted in the sauce as it is cooked.

Tabasco sauce

you will need	1 teaspoon dry mustard
	¼ pint tomato juice
	1 tablespoon vinegar
	2 tablespoons soft brown sugar
	1 tablespoon oil
	1 tablespoon lemon juice
	salt and pepper
	1 small onion
	1 teaspoon tabasco sauce
equipment	*shallow bowl and spoon*
	measuring jug
	teaspoon
	tablespoon
	knife and chopping board

Mix the mustard with the tomato juice — the liquid from tinned tomatoes will do very well. Then add the vinegar, sugar, oil, lemon juice, salt and pepper to taste and chopped onion, and stir well. Lastly add the tabasco. It is very hot and 1 teaspoon may be too much for your taste.

Use as a basting sauce.

Note

When barbecuing roasts or poultry on the spit, we advise applying the sauce generously during the last few minutes of the barbecuing period. Besides adding flavour, it keeps the meat moist and appetising; and when applied in this way, you taste the sauce and the meat separately.

195

Burgundy marinade

you will need	$\frac{1}{4}$ teaspoon dry mustard
	2 tablespoons lemon juice
	2 cloves garlic
	1 small onion
	1 stick celery
	6 tablespoons olive oil
	4 tablespoons red Burgundy
	salt and pepper
equipment	*bowl and spoon*
	knife and chopping board
	tablespoon
	teaspoon

Mix mustard with the lemon juice. Chop garlic, onion and celery very finely, and mix thoroughly with all the other ingredients. Leave for several hours if possible before using.

Use as a marinade for beef kebabs, and baste with the sauce while the kebabs are cooking.

Cider and lemon marinade

you will need	juice 1 lemon
	4 tablespoons cider
	salt and pepper
	1 teaspoon crushed rosemary
equipment	*bowl and spoon*
	tablespoon
	teaspoon

Mix all together in the bowl and use to marinade the meat overnight.

196

Garlic butter

you will need	4 oz. butter
	2 cloves garlic
	salt and pepper
equipment	*bowl*
	knife and chopping board
	wooden spoon

Work the butter slightly, to soften, then pound in the finely chopped garlic, the salt and plenty of freshly ground black pepper.

For Garlic bread:—

Slice a loaf (the largest that will fit into your biggest saucepan), nearly through, leaving it joined at the bottom. Spread the garlic butter between the slices, wrap it all in metal foil and place on another piece of crumpled foil in the pan. Make the whole thing really hot until the garlic butter melts into the bread and the crust is even crustier.

Ideally this should be done with French bread, but a pan that shape is such an unhandy thing in camp or afloat.

Note

Garlic butter can be used, as above, for garlic bread, and for basting meats. It can also be used in vegetable dishes, and is excellent with spinach; heat about 2 oz. garlic butter in a frying pan and add 2 lb. cooked, well drained spinach with salt and pepper to taste. Heat, stirring for 2 minutes. Then sprinkle with lemon juice and serve.

Vanilla sauce

you will need
1 small can evaporated milk
1 tablespoon cornflour
1 tablespoon castor sugar
½ oz. butter
1 teaspoon vanilla essence

equipment
saucepan
measuring jug
can opener
tablespoon
teaspoon
wooden spoon
knife

Put the evaporated milk into the measuring jug and make up to ¾ pint with water. Pour most of the milk into the saucepan but leave enough to blend with the cornflour. Add sugar to the milk in the saucepan, bring to the boil and pour on to the blended cornflour, stirring. Return to the pan and cook for 2 − 3 minutes, stirring all the time. Stir in the butter and vanilla essence and serve immediately.

Syrup or honey sauce

you will need
8 oz. syrup or honey
¾ pint water
rind and juice 1 lemon or pinch ground ginger

equipment
small saucepan
wooden spoon
grater and lemon squeezer

Stir the syrup or honey and the water together until smooth. Add the lemon or ginger and serve hot.

Caramel sauce

you will need
4 oz. demerara sugar
4 tablespoons cold water
½ large can evaporated milk
1 dessertspoon cornflour

equipment
saucepan
wooden spoon
can opener
small bowl or jug
dessertspoon

Put the sugar with 3 tablespoons water over a low heat and dissolve carefully. Bring to the boil and cook until the mixture is thick and sticky. Add the evaporated milk and stir over the heat until the caramel dissolves into the warm milk. Mix the cornflour in the bowl with the rest of the water, pour the milk mixture on to it, stirring, return to the pan and boil for 2 minutes. Delicious with vanilla ice cream.

Cream whip

you will need
1 egg white
1 teaspoon sugar
6 oz. can cream
2 drops vanilla essence

equipment
small bowl or jug
egg whisk or fork
teaspoon
can opener

Whisk the egg white until stiff, add the sugar and whisk again. Fold in the cream and stir in the essence.

This method not only disguises the taste of the can but makes the cream go further.

Chocolate sauce

you will need   4 oz. grated plain chocolate
                         4 oz. castor sugar
                         1 small can evaporated milk

equipment   *double saucepan or heatproof bowl*
                         or jug and saucepan
                         grater or potato peeler
                         can opener
                         wooden spoon

Put all the ingredients into the bowl or the top of the double saucepan. Stir until the sugar and chocolate have dissolved and the sauce thickens. Good hot or cold with ice cream.

Apricot sauce

you will need   2 level teaspoons arrowroot
                         $\frac{1}{2}$ pint syrup from the fruit
                         little sugar
                         2 tablespoons lemon juice
                         8 oz. canned or cooked apricots

equipment   *teaspoon*
                         tablespoon
                         wooden spoon
                         saucepan

Blend the arrowroot with a little of the syrup from the can of fruit or the cooked fruit. Put it into a saucepan with the lemon juice and sugar to taste.

Bring to the boil and cook until thickened and quite clear. Add the halved apricots and heat gently. Add more sugar if wished.

Delicious served with steamed puddings, ice cream etc.

Butterscotch sauce

you will need	2 oz. brown sugar
	1 tablespoon golden syrup
	1 oz. butter
	4 tablespoons water
equipment	*tablespoon*
	wooden spoon
	saucepan

Put the sugar, syrup and butter into a saucepan. Cook on a gentle heat, and stir until the sugar has dissolved. Bring to the boil and allow to boil steadily for a few minutes. Add the water and bring back to the boil. Cook steadily until the water has blended with the ingredients.

Cold brandy sauce

you will need	2 eggs
	$\frac{1}{2}$ pint milk
	2 oz. sugar
	2 tablespoons brandy
equipment	*tablespoon*
	wooden spoon
	saucepan
	bowl
	fork or whisk

Beat the egg yolks with the milk and put into a saucepan with the sugar and brandy. Cook gently until thick enough to coat the back of a wooden spoon. Allow to cool, stirring from time to time.

Just before serving fold in the stiffly beaten egg whites.

Puddings

My family maintain that no meal is complete without a sweet course. And since there are really few puddings that are impossible to produce in camp or afloat, there is really no reason why they shouldn't have them.

We always take an apple pie for supper on the first night. Then if the trip is an extended one I bake one or two flan cases (of varying sizes so that they nest) to be filled as required.

A lot of the recipes in this section are for fruit puddings, since we always hope that the weather will be ideal and these are the sort of things we shall want. But there are also a few heavier recipes, which can be very comforting if the weather should be awful, and useful if the main course has been a light one.

Fruit cup
To serve 4

you will need	$\frac{1}{4}$ pint water
	4 oz. sugar
	1 small punnet strawberries
	1 small punnet raspberries
	2 bananas, sliced
	whipped cream or
	cream whip, see page 199
equipment	*saucepan*
	serving dish
	knife

Boil the water and sugar together for 3 minutes and leave to get cool. Hull the strawberries and mix with the other fruit. Pour the syrup over and leave for as long as possible before serving. Serve with cream and sponge fingers.

Fruit salad

you will need	½ pint water
	2 oz. sugar
	2 oranges
	2 apples
	1 pear
	bunch of grapes
	2 bananas
	8 oz. ripe plums
	lemon juice
equipment	*saucepan*
	sharp knife
	board
	cup
	serving dish

Boil the water and sugar with the peel of 1 of the oranges cut into strips. Leave to cool. Meanwhile prepare all the fruit, dropping the banana slices and the pieces of apple briefly into lemon juice to preserve the colour.

Mix all together in the serving dish, if possible several hours before needed.

Banana split

To serve 4

you will need	4 ripe bananas
	1 small block vanilla ice cream
	chocolate sauce, see page 200
	chopped nuts
equipment	*knife*
	4 small serving dishes

Cut each banana in 2 and sandwich together with ice cream. Pour the chocolate sauce over and decorate with chopped nuts.

Strawberries in yoghourt

To serve 4

you will need	1 lb. strawberries
	$\frac{1}{4}$ pint double cream
	1 carton plain yoghourt
	1 egg white
	2 oz. castor sugar
equipment	*shallow serving dish*
	jug and fork or whisk
	bowl

Put the strawberries into the serving dish.

Whisk the cream until stiff, mix in the yoghourt and fold in the stiffly beaten egg white and the sugar. Pour over the strawberries.

Strawberry milk jelly

To serve 4

you will need	1 strawberry jelly
	1 small can evaporated milk
	bananas to decorate, if liked
equipment	*measuring jug*
	wooden spoon
	can opener
	serving dish
	knife

Dissolve the jelly in enough very hot water to cover. Make up to $\frac{3}{4}$ pint with cold water. When the jelly is on the point of setting, whisk in enough evaporated milk to make up to 1 pint, or slightly less in hot weather. Whisk well and turn in to serving dish to set. Slice bananas over the top just before serving.

Ambrosia

To serve 4

you will need	3 large bananas
	3 oranges
	2 tablespoons soft brown sugar
	2 tablespoons desiccated coconut
equipment	*knife*
	serving dish
	tablespoon

Peel and slice the bananas and peel the oranges and divide into segments, removing all the pith. Mix together with the sugar in the serving dish and sprinkle the top with coconut. Serve immediately.

Banana and chocolate cream

To serve 4

you will need	4 bananas
	2 tablespoons castor sugar
	6 oz. can cream
	juice 1 lemon
	2 oz. bar plain chocolate
	glacé cherries, optional
equipment	*fork*
	mixing bowl
	tablespoon
	can opener
	sharp knife
	lemon squeezer
	serving dish
	grater or potato peeler

Mash the bananas in the bowl with the sugar. Mix in the cream and then the lemon juice. Turn into the serving dish and sprinkle with the grated chocolate and, if liked, decorate with glacé cherries.

Prune and banana whip

To serve 4

you will need	8 oz. dried prunes
	1 packet black currant jelly
	2 bananas
equipment	*saucepan*
	serving dish
	measuring jug
	whisk or fork
	knife

Soak the prunes for several hours in just enough water to cover.

Cook them gently for 15—20 minutes until tender. When they are cooked pour the liquid on to the jelly and stir until dissolved.

Make up to a scant pint with cold water, using less water in very hot weather.

When the jelly has reached the syrupy stage whisk until light and fluffy.

Put a layer of sliced banana in the serving dish, then one of stoned, chopped prunes, and cover with a layer of jelly. Repeat 1—2 times, finishing with the jelly, and serve with fresh cream or Cream whip, see page 199.

Bananas with yoghourt

To serve 4

you will need	6 bananas
	1 oz. almonds
	2 tablespoons soft brown sugar
	1 carton plain yoghourt
equipment	*knife and board*
	jug
	spoon
	serving dish

Slice the bananas and then chop them roughly. Blanch and peel the almonds, chop them, and add them with the sugar to the bananas. Mix in the yoghourt and serve.

Bondi glory

To serve 4

you will need	1 pineapple jelly
	1 medium-sized can pineapple pieces
	1 orange jelly
	1 egg white
	6 oz. can cream or fresh cream
	few glacé cherries
equipment	*heatproof measuring jug*
	wooden spoon
	can opener
	large serving dish
	egg whisk or fork

Dissolve the pineapple jelly in enough hot water to cover. Pour in the juice from the tin of pineapple and make the liquid up to 1 pint with cold water. Put the pineapple pieces in the serving dish and pour the jelly over and allow to set.

Dissolve the orange jelly in 1 pint hot water—less if the weather is hot—and add to the serving dish. Leave to set.

Give the can of cream to someone to shake thoroughly, or whisk the fresh cream, while you whisk the egg white until stiff in the measuring jug.

Then fold in the cream, spread on top of the jelly and decorate with glacé cherries.

Pineapple pan pudding

To serve 4

you will need	5 oz. margarine
	2 oz. soft brown sugar
	4 rings canned pineapple
	3 oz. sugar
	2 beaten eggs
	4 oz. self-raising flour
	good pinch salt
equipment	*large heavy frying pan and lid*
	can opener
	mixing bowl
	wooden spoon
	small bowl for egg
	fork or whisk
	asbestos mat

Mix together 2 oz. of the margarine and the brown sugar in the frying pan. Melt but do not let the mixture boil. Lay the drained pineapple in the pan.

Cream the rest of the margarine with the sugar until white and smooth, stir in the beaten eggs and then the flour and salt. Spread over the pineapple rings, cover the pan tightly and cook on the lowest heat possible for 30 minutes.

Turn on to a plate to serve so that the pineapple will be on top, and serve with cream or Cream whip, see page 199.

Rhubarb jelly

To serve 4

you will need   8 oz. rhubarb
1 packet raspberry flavoured jelly
6 oz. sugar

equipment   *knife and board*
measuring jug
wooden spoon
mould or serving dish

Wash the rhubarb and cut into 1-inch pieces. Put into the saucepan, pour on boiling water and leave for 5 minutes to reduce the acidity. Meanwhile, disolve the jelly in a small amount of hot water. Cook the drained rhubarb, in enough water to cover, until tender but still whole, then add the sugar. Add enough of the rhubarb and juice to the jelly to make up to 1 pint, then turn into the mould or dish to set.

I usually let mine cool a bit, then turn it into a plastic container with a lid. It doesn't exactly make for dainty presentation, but it's awfully convenient.

Peach marshmallow

To serve 4

you will need   1 medium-sized can sliced peaches
6 oz. marshmallows

equipment   *fireproof dish*
can opener

Turn the peaches into the serving dish, strew the marshmallows over the top and put under the grill until pale golden brown.

Only for the sweet-toothed.

Plum fool

you will need	1 lb. Victoria plums
	3 oz. sugar
	$\frac{1}{2}$ pint whipped cream or
	$\frac{1}{2}$ pint thick custard
	few drops red colouring optional
equipment	*saucepan and lid*
	jug or bowl
	nylon sieve
	wooden spoon
	tablespoon

Cook the plums very gently in a small amount of water, and when they are soft add the sugar to taste. Rub through a sieve, allow to get quite cold, and mix with the cream or custard. Add a few drops of colouring if necessary.

Peaches and raspberries

you will need	1 lb. ripe peaches
	1 punnet raspberries
	2 oz. sugar
equipment	*knife*
	saucepan boiling water
	serving dish

Dip the peaches in boiling water for a moment, skin them and cut in half, removing the stones. Put them in the serving dish, scatter the raspberries over them and sprinkle them with sugar.

Peach and banana gâteau

To serve 4−5

you will need	1 sponge square, see page 244
	2 bananas
	1 small can sliced peaches
	$\frac{1}{4}$ pint fresh cream or Cream whip, see page 199
equipment	*knife*
	serving dish
	can opener
	fork or whisk
	jug

Slice the sponge square through the middle and put $\frac{1}{2}$ in the serving dish.

Slice half a banana over it, then spread over some of the peaches and a little of the juice.

Spread $\frac{1}{3}$ of the cream in the centre, put the top half of the sponge and press well down.

Make some slits in the top half of the sponge and carefully pour on some of the fruit juice.

Coat with the remainder of the cream and pile the rest of the peaches on top with the bananas round the edge.

Variation

Apricot halves can replace the peaches, and to add colour and flavour decorate with canned cherries.

Lemon mousse

you will need	6 oz. sugar
	1 pint milk
	$\frac{1}{2}$ oz gelatine
	2 lemons
	2 eggs, separated
	whipped fresh cream or Cream whip, see page 199
equipment	*lemon squeezer*
	saucepan
	bowl or jug for egg whites
	grater
	wooden spoon
	fork or whisk
	mould or sundae glasses

Put sugar, milk, gelatine and finely grated lemon rind into a pan.

Heat slowly until sugar dissolves, then add the egg yolks and boil until the milk curdles.

Allow to cool. Whisk the egg whites until stiff and add them with the lemon juice to the milk mixture. Pour into a mould or individual dishes and leave to set.

Serve with whipped fresh cream or Cream whip.

Variation

For an orange mouse, instead of the juice of two lemons, use the juice of one orange and half a lemon. Use the finely grated orange rind.

Summer pudding

you will need	2 lb. mixed soft fruit — raspberries, gooseberries cherries, red and black currants, blackberries ¼ pint water 6 oz. sugar thin slices white bread fresh cream or Cream whip, see page 199
equipment	*fork and knife* *saucepan* *basin* *plate* *heavy weight*

Strip the currants from the stalks, top and tail the gooseberries and stone the cherries. Mix all the washed fruit together and simmer gently with the water and the sugar until soft.

Cut the crusts off the bread and line the basin with it. Fill carefully with the fruit, reserving some of the juice. Cover the top of the pudding with bread and pour the rest of the juice on to it. Put the plate on top and weight it. Leave overnight.

Turn out the pudding and serve with fresh cream or Cream whip.

Raspberry trifle

you will need	4 sponge cakes
	1 medium-sized can raspberries
	1 pint milk
	2 oz. sugar
	3 bananas
	2 tablespoons custard powder
	6 oz. can cream
	1 egg white
	1 teaspoon castor sugar
equipment	*knife*
	1 serving dish
	can opener
	wooden spoon
	saucepan for custard
	jug or bowl for custard
	fork or whisk
	teaspoon

Split the sponge cakes and arrange them round the base of the serving dish. Put the milk, except for two tablespoons to boil with the sugar.

Open the raspberries and pour into the serving dish, and slice 2 bananas over them. Make the custard and allow to cool a little, then pour carefully over the bananas and raspberries.

Leave until quite cold. When the trifle is needed, whisk the egg white until stiff, fold in the canned cream and castor sugar, and spread over the custard. Decorate with the remaining banana, sliced.

Variation

Use ½ pint raspberry jelly and ½ pint custard, instead of 1 pint custard. This means reducing the milk to ½ pint. Use juice from the fruit to make the jelly, made up to ½ pint with water. Pour custard on the fruit first, and then the jelly, whipped-up when set. Then cream etc.

Blackberry jelly

you will need
8 oz. blackberries
½ pint water
4 oz. sugar
¾ oz. gelatine dissolved in ¼ pint water
whipped cream or Cream whip, see page 199

equipment
saucepan
wooden spoon
measuring jug
serving bowl or mould
sieve

Stew together the washed fruit, ½ pint water and sugar to taste. When the fruit is soft, sieve it and add the dissolved gelatine. Make the liquid up to 1 pint or a little less if the weather is hot.

When set, serve with whipped cream or Cream whip.

Bilberry tapioca

To serve 4

you will need
1 punnet bilberries
3 oz. sugar or to taste
2 oz. fine tapioca
2 oz. sugar
2 eggs, separated
1 oz. sugar

equipment
heatproof serving dish
saucepan and lid
small bowl or jug
fork or whisk

Stew the bilberries with sugar to taste and very little water until soft. Turn into serving dish and leave to cool.

Rinse the pan and cook the tapioca in ½ pint water until clear. Add 2 oz. sugar and yolks of egg. Whip well and add carefully to the dish.

Whip the egg whites until stiff and fold in the 1 oz. sugar. Spread over the tapioca, leaving the surface smooth.

Light the grill. (Do not pre-heat.) Put the serving dish underneath and watch it carefully. The moment the meringue begins to turn colour, turn the grill off, but leave the pudding where it is until quite cold.

Peach Melba
To serve 4

you will need	1 family block vanilla ice cream
	1 medium-sized can peaches
	1 medium-sized can raspberries
	4 heaped tablespoons icing sugar
equipment	*4 small dishes*
	can opener
	tablespoon
	strainer
	wooden spoon

Divide the ice cream into 4 and put one portion into each dish. Drain the peaches and arrange round the ice cream. Rub the raspberries through the sieve and mix with the icing sugar until the sauce is of a pouring consistency, then pour over each portion of ice cream and peaches.

Strawberry orange

you will need	1 large punnet strawberries juice 1 orange 2 oz. castor sugar fresh whipped cream
equipment	*serving dish* *lemon squeezer* *spoon* *knife*

Hull the strawberries and mix with the orange juice and sugar to taste. Leave for at least 1 hour before serving. Top with whipped cream.

Pear condé

you will need	1 small can pears 3 level teaspoons cornflour few drops red colouring, optional 1 can cooked rice pudding
equipment	*measuring jug* *small pan* *can opener* *teaspoon* *wooden spoon* *serving dish*

Measure $\frac{1}{4}$ pint of juice from the canned pears. Mix with the cornflour and bring to the boil. Cook very gently for 3–4 minutes. Add red colouring if liked. Turn the rice pudding into the dish, arrange the pears on top and glaze with the sauce.

Steamed ginger pudding

you will need	2 oz. shredded suet
	4 oz. plain flour
	2 teaspoons baking powder
	1 oz. sugar
	pinch salt
	1 teaspoon ground ginger
	1 egg
	1 good tablespoon syrup
	¼ pint milk
equipment	*mixing bowl*
	tablespoon
	teaspoon
	pudding basin
	metal foil
	large saucepan and lid

Mix together in the mixing bowl the suet, flour, baking powder, sugar, salt and ginger. Make a well in the centre and add the beaten egg and mix well. Then mix in the syrup and the milk. Steam in the pudding basin firmly covered with metal foil for 1½ hours, or longer if possible.

Delicious served with apricot sauce, see page 200.

Variation

Try this pudding topped with marmalade. Put a round of greased greaseproof paper in the basin first, then two tablespoons of marmalade, and then the pudding mixture. Steam it for at least 1½ hours. The marmalade will give the pudding an attractive moist top when it is turned out of the basin, and it combines well with the ginger flavour.

Chocolate apple pudding

To serve 4

you will need
1 large can apple purée
¼ pint double cream or Cream whip, see page 199
2 oz. plain chocolate

equipment
can opener
serving dish
jug and fork or whisk
grater or potato peeler

Put the apple purée in the dish and cover with the whipped cream or Cream whip. Grate chocolate decoratively over the top.

Toffee plum pudding

To serve 4

you will need
2 oz. butter
8 oz. soft brown sugar
2 tablespoons lemon juice
3½-inch slices cut from large loaf
1 lb. plums
¼ pint fresh double cream or Cream whip, see page 199

equipment
frying pan and lid
tablespoon
lemon squeezer
wooden spoon
sharp knife
bread board

Melt the butter, add the sugar and heat slowly until the sugar dissolves, then stir in the lemon juice. Cut the crusts off the slices of bread and cut into $\frac{3}{4}$-inch squares, then fold the squares gently through the toffee mixture until they are all evenly coated. Add the plums, stoned and cut into 4. Cover the pan and cook until the plums are soft.

Serve with cream or Cream whip when quite cold.

For the sweet-toothed.

Danish apple cake

To serve 4

you will need	2 oz. butter
	6 oz. breadcrumbs
	1 teaspoon cinnamon
	2 oz. sugar
	2 tablespoons cornflour
	1 medium-sized can sweetened apple sauce
equipment	*2 saucepans*
	serving dish
	wooden spoon
	tablespoon
	can opener

Melt the butter in a pan, add the breadcrumbs, cinnamon and sugar and brown over a low heat, stirring constantly. In the other pan, mix the cornflour with 2 tablespoons water until smooth, then add the apple sauce. Mix well and boil for 3 minutes, stirring constantly.

Put the crumb mixture and the apple sauce in the serving dish in layers, ending with the crumbs. Put in a cool place for at least an hour before serving with custard, ice cream or evaporated milk.

Blackberry and apple suet pudding

To serve 4

you will need	8 oz. blackberries
	1 lb. cooking apples
	4 oz. sugar
	4 oz. self-raising flour
	2 oz. shredded suet
	pinch salt
	water to mix
equipment	*saucepan and lid*
	fork
	sharp knife
	potato peeler
	mixing bowl
	blunt knife

Cook the washed blackberries in enough water to cover until tender.

Mash them against the side of the saucepan, pour the juice into the bowl and throw away the seeds.

Peel and quarter the apples and put them in the rinsed saucepan with the blackberrry juice and sugar to taste. Bring to the boil.

Mix the flour and shredded suet with the salt in the clean mixing bowl, add enough water to make a stiff dough, form into a ball between floured palms and flatten to make a round which exactly fits the saucepan. Place on top of the apples, put the lid firmly on the pan, and cook fairly fast without removing the lid for 25 minutes.

Serve with custard, cream or ice cream.

Jam ping-pongs

To serve 4

you will need	8 oz. self-raising flour
	4 oz. shredded suet
	pinch salt
	water to mix
	raspberry jam
equipment	*bowl for mixing*
	blunt knife for mixing
	saucepan
	wooden skewer or something
	similar for inserting jam
	teaspoon
	draining spoon

Mix the flour and suet together in the bowl and add enough water to make a rather stiff dough. Roll between floured palms to form balls the size of a ping-pong ball, make a little tunnel to the centre of each one and insert some jam, sealing it over afterwards. Cook in boiling water for about 15 minutes and serve with whipped cream or ice cream.

Butterscotch tart

To serve 4

you will need	double quantity Caramel sauce, see page 199
	1 7-inch pastry shell
	chopped nuts
equipment	*spoon*
	knife

Pour the caramel sauce while still warm into the pastry shell, smooth the top and decorate with chopped nuts.

Manchester tart

you will need	2 tablespoons raspberry jam
	1 cooked pastry shell
	4 tablespoons apple purée, tinned or fresh
	1 tablespoon custard powder
	½ pint milk
	1 oz. sugar
equipment	*tablespoon*
	can opener
	saucepan
	wooden spoon
	bowl
	serving plate

Spread the jam evenly over the pastry shell and pour the apple purée over it.

Make the custard, using a scant ½ pint milk, which can be fresh, diluted evaporated, or reconstituted dried milk. When the custard has cooled to blood heat, pour it gently into the flan case and allow to get quite cold before serving.

Cherry flan

To serve 4

you will need	1 medium-sized can cherries
	1 cooked pastry shell
	2 level dessertspoons cornflour
	fresh cream or Cream whip, see page 199
equipment	*can opener*
	small pan
	measuring jug
	dessertspoon
	wooden spoon

Drain the cherries and arrange in the pastry shell. Measure ⅓ pint of juice from the can and mix with the cornflour.

Bring to the boil and boil for 3 – 4 minutes. Pour over the cherries and allow to cool.

Serve with fresh cream or Cream whip.

Variation

Most soft fruits make delightful flan fillings. If using canned fruits the juice can be drained off and thickened with a little jelly with the same flavour. Pour this on to the fruit in the flan just before it sets. Try mandarin oranges with an orange jelly.

Tarte de miel

To serve 4

you will need	3 oz. margarine
	3 oz. castor sugar
	1 tablespoon honey
	3 oz. ground almonds
	1 cooked pastry case
	6 oz. icing sugar
	3 dessertspoons warm water
	few drops lemon juice
	chopped nuts
equipment	*bowl for mixing*
	fork
	tablespoon
	knife

Cream the margarine and sugar together until soft and fluffy. Work in the honey and almonds, then spread the mixture evenly over the flan case. Mix the icing sugar and water vigorously until smooth, add a few drops of lemon juice, stirring, then pour on to the mixture in the pastry case. Decorate with chopped nuts and allow to set firm before serving.

Banana cream pie

To serve 4

you will need	2 bananas 1 7-inch cooked pastry case 1 family block vanilla ice cream ½ pint milk ½ tablespoon custard powder 1 oz. sugar
equipment	*fairly large bowl* *tablespoon* *knife*

Slice the bananas and send someone off to buy a block of ice cream while you make the custard. Arrange the bananas over the pastry, and when the custard has cooled chop the ice cream roughly into it. Pile on to the bananas and top with a few more. Serve immediately.

Rosy apple custard

To serve 4

you will need	2½ level tablespoons custard powder 1 pint milk 2 tablespoons rose hip syrup 4 rosy eating apples a little lemon juice
equipment	*tablespoon* *wooden spoon* *bowl* *saucepan*

Mix custard powder to a thin, smooth paste with the cold milk, pour into a pan and cook, stirring, until custard comes to the boil and thickens. Simmer 2 minutes, remove from heat then blend in the rose hip syrup. Coarsely grate 3 unpeeled, but well washed, apples, add to custard then transfer mixture to 4 small dishes. Leave until cold and just before serving, decorate top of each with 4 thin slices of unpeeled apple (first dipped in lemon juice to prevent browning).

Honey soufflé omelette To serve 4

you will need	1 dessert apple
	2 tablespoons honey
	2 eggs separated
	1 teaspoon castor sugar
	$\frac{1}{4}$ teaspoon vanilla essence
	$\frac{1}{2}$ oz. butter
equipment	*chopping board and knife*
	tablespoon
	wooden spoon
	bowl
	saucepan
	frying pan

Peel, core and slice apple thinly. Place in a small saucepan with the honey. Heat gently and keep warm. Beat up yolks with castor sugar and vanilla essence. Fold into the stiffly whisked egg whites. Melt the butter in the frying pan, if possible a 6-inch omelette pan, and when hot pour in the egg mixture. Cook for one minute over gentle heat, finishing under a grill, or if there is no grill turn quickly, and cook for another minute. Cut across centre quickly, and place honey and apple mixture on one half of omelette, fold over the other half, slide on to a hot plate, or sprinkle with castor sugar.

Variation

To make a lemon soufflé omelette omit the apple and honey and when the omelette is risen and set a golden brown, turn it out on to a warm dish. Make an incision across the centre with a sharp knife, spread with about 2 tablespoons of lemon cheese, fold over, dredge with castor sugar and serve immediately.

Melon en surprise

To serve 4–6

you will need	1 honeydew melon
	2 dessertspoons clear honey
	2 dessertspoons lemon juice
	1 small can mandarin oranges
	1 small can cherries
	1 family block vanilla ice cream
equipment	*sharp knife*
	chopping board
	dessertspoon
	shallow bowl

Cut a slice from one side of the melon making zig-zag cuts. Scoop out the melon flesh and cut into small cubes. Mix with the honey and lemon juice. Drain juice from fruit and remove the cherry stones. Mix fruit with the diced melon. Put a layer of fruit into the melon shell. Cover with ice cream. Pile remaining fruit on top. Garnish with sprigs of fresh mint. The juice from the fruit can be used to make Jelly mousse, see page 229.

Honey junket

To serve 4

you will need	4 teaspoons clear honey
	1 pint milk
	3 teaspoons essence of rennet
	2–3 drops vanilla essence
equipment	*saucepan*
	serving bowl

Warm the honey over a gentle heat until runny. Add milk and vanilla and stir until lukewarm. Stir in the rennet. Pour at once into a serving bowl. When set, dust a little grated nutmeg over the top if liked.

Jelly mousse

To serve 4

you will need	½ pint fruit juice or water
	1 packet lemon jelly
	1 small can evaporated milk
	juice of ½ lemon
	1 dessertspoon lemon curd
equipment	*saucepan*
	fork or whisk

Bring fruit juice to the boil. Take off the heat and stir in the jelly until dissolved. Allow to cool. Whisk evaporated milk until thick. Add lemon juice and lemon curd and whisk again until it peaks. When jelly is quite cold whisk until light and frothy. Add jelly to whipped milk, whisking all the time. Pour into a bowl and decorate with whipped cream and fruit.

Lemon foam pudding

To serve 4

you will need	3 oranges
	1 lemon
	3 eggs
	4 teaspoons sugar
	2 teaspoons cornflour
equipment	*bowl*
	saucepan
	lemon squeezer

Squeeze the juice from the fruit and make it up to ½ pint, if necessary, with water. Separate the yolks from whites of eggs. Put egg yolks together with sugar, cornflour and the fruit juice in a saucepan. Add the grated rind of the lemon. Cook over a gentle heat, stirring. Just bring to the boil, sufficient to let it thicken. Beat the egg whites stiffly, and fold in to sauce. Can be served warm or cold.

Scones, cakes, teabreads and biscuits

Even if you normally have little appetite for cakes and other sweet things, when you are spending the whole day in the open air there are times when a good slab of home made cake goes down very well indeed.

The recipes for cakes in this section have been chosen because they keep well, and there are also recipes for drop scones and other bread substitutes which can be produced quite quickly on a frying pan or griddle.

To keep cakes fresh and moist; store carefully in a separate container from bread, biscuits or pastry. Wrap them in foil or greaseproof paper.

Take care not to overcook cakes you are wanting to keep for some time, and do not omit the golden syrup if this is an ingredient in a cake recipe, it helps to keep it very moist for quite a long time. If a fruit cake becomes a little dry it can be sliced thinly and buttered, and served as rich tea bread.

We have not listed the equipment needed for cake making, since this will depend on what you use at home.

Successful cake making depends on the way you handle the ingredients. Weigh them carefully. Follow the recipe exactly for the first time, before you make any modifications. Remember, also, that oven temperatures vary, so check yours with those given in the manufacturer's instruction book, and happy baking!

Potato cakes

you will need	½ pint and 4 tablespoons water
	1 level teaspoon salt
	3½ oz. packet instant potato
	4 oz. margarine
	6 oz. self-raising flour
	pepper
	butter
equipment	*saucepan*
	teaspoon
	fork
	board
	griddle or large frying pan
	teacloth

Put the water and salt to boil in the saucepan. Remove from the heat and mix in the instant potato. When well mixed, add the margarine, cut in small pieces. Then fork in flour and pepper to taste. Mix well.

Allow to become quite cold. Flour the board, take ½ the potato mixture and form into a smooth ball between floured hands, then flatten on the board to a round about 6-inches across. Cut into 8 and fry on a moderately hot, lightly buttered griddle until brown underneath, then turn and cook the other side. Repeat with the other half.

Serve warm with butter. Keep until ready to use wrapped in a teacloth.

Variation

These can be made with fresh potatoes, in which case you take 1 lb. boiled potatoes, 4 oz. flour, teaspoon baking powder, pinch of salt, 1 egg, 1 oz. melted butter. Mix all these ingredients together. Flatten on a floured board, shape into rounds and cook as above.

Oatmeal bannocks

you will need	6 oz. flour
	2 teaspoons baking powder
	¼ teaspoon salt
	4 oz. margarine
	8 level tablespoons oatmeal
	2 teaspoons sugar
	¼ pint milk
	little fat for frying
equipment	*mixing bowl*
	fork
	teaspoon
	tablespoon
	large frying pan or griddle

Mix the flour with the baking powder and salt and rub in the fat with a fork. Stir in the oatmeal and sugar, make a well in the centre and add enough milk to make a soft dough. Break off pieces of dough, roll between the palms (flour them first) and flatten to make cakes about ½-inch thick. Fry on a moderately hot greased griddle or frying pan.

These bannocks are very good with butter and marmalade when you run out of bread far from the beaten track.

Variation

Oatmeal and potato bannocks can be made by substituting the 6 oz. flour with 4 oz. mashed potato and 2 oz. flour. Use one egg and half the amount of milk given for binding the ingredients together. Make the cakes as above, and fry on a hot greased griddle, or cook in an oven, if available, on a greased tin.

Welsh griddle cakes

you will need	6 oz. plain flour
	1½ oz. sugar
	pinch salt
	½ level teaspoon bicarbonate soda
	1 tablespoon cream tartar
	dissolved in water
	3 tablespoons sour cream
	scant ¼ pint milk
	butter for frying
equipment	*mixing bowl*
	wooden spoon
	tablespoon
	teaspoon
	griddle or large frying pan
	fish slice

Mix all the ingredients together in the mixing bowl, beat well and allow to stand for a little. Grease the frying pan or griddle and drop spoonfuls of the mixture on to it when it is moderately hot. When the underneath of each griddle cake is brown and bubbles begin to appear on top, flip over and cook the other side.

Eat hot with butter and jam.

Variation

These griddle cakes can have currants and spice added for a change. Add 2 oz. of currants and ¼ teaspoon mixed spice into the well beaten mixture, and cook as instructions given above.

Drop scones

you will need
2 oz. margarine
2 tablespoons boiling water
1 egg
$\frac{3}{8}$ pint evaporated milk
4 oz. self-raising flour
$\frac{1}{2}$ teaspoon salt
$1\frac{1}{2}$ teaspoons baking powder
2 teaspoons sugar

equipment
large mixing bowl
small bowl
cup and fork
can opener
teaspoon
wooden spoon
tablespoon
large frying pan or griddle
tea towel
fish slice

Put the margarine into the small bowl, pour on the boiling water and stir until melted. Beat the egg and add it with the evaporated milk to the margarine. Stir well. Mix the flour, salt, baking powder and sugar in the large bowl and add the milk mixture all at once, stirring briskly until well mixed.

Leave the mixture for 30 minutes before using, if possible, then cook a tablespoon at a time in the hot, lightly greased frying pan. If you are using a griddle you can cook several together. Turn them when they are brown underneath and bubbles appear on the surface, and keep warm until needed in the cloth.

Eat hot with butter and jam, or with bacon.

Batter cakes

you will need	4 oz. plain flour
	good pinch salt
	1 egg
	¼ pint milk
	little butter
equipment	*bowl for mixing*
	wooden spoon
	tablespoon
	frying pan or griddle
	fish slice or spatula

Put the flour and salt into the mixing bowl, make a well in the centre and drop the egg in. Beat well and add the milk by degrees, beating until smooth. Allow to stand for an hour if possible before using.

Drop in spoonfuls on to a moderately hot greased griddle, allowing plenty of room between as the batter cakes spread. Turn when browned underneath. If you are using a frying pan it will be quicker to cook large ones which nearly fill the pan.

You will probably find that these are so popular that you need twice the above quantity.

THESE CAKES WILL KEEP AND CAN BE MADE AT HOME

Survival cake

you will need 12 oz. self-raising flour
$\frac{1}{4}$ teaspoon nutmeg
$\frac{1}{4}$ teaspoon cinnamon
$\frac{1}{2}$ teaspoon mixed spice
grated rind $\frac{1}{2}$ lemon
$2\frac{1}{4}$ oz. margarine
6 oz. brown sugar
1 lb. mixed dried fruit
1 oz. peel
1 oz. cherries
$\frac{1}{2}$ pint cider or fruit juice
$\frac{3}{4}$ teaspoon bicarbonate of soda
1 tablespoon milk

Sieve flour and spices and add finely grated lemon rind. Rub in margarine and add sugar and fruit. Make a well in the centre of the mixture, pour in the cider or juice followed by the bicarbonate dissolved in the milk. Stir well and turn into 8-inch cake tin.

Leave in the tin for 12 hours, then bake in a moderate oven (350°F. – Gas Mark 4) for about $1\frac{1}{2}$ hours or until a knife comes out clean.

Very comforting with a mug of chocolate in a Force 8 gale.

Cherry and almond cake

you will need
8 oz. margarine
8 oz. sugar
10 oz. plain flour
½ teaspoon baking powder
pinch salt
3 eggs
2 oz. ground almonds
few drops almond essence

Cream the margarine and sugar until very white and fluffy, then stir in the sieved plain flour, baking powder and salt alternately with the beaten eggs. Then add the ground almonds and a few drops of almond essence.

Bake in a tin 10 × 8 × 2½ inches for 3 hours in a very slow oven (250°F. – Gas Mark ½).

Keep for 2 weeks before using.

Moist cherry cake

you will need
6 oz. margarine
6 oz. sugar
3 eggs
8 oz. self-raising flour
pinch salt
1 teaspoon baking powder
4 tablespoons milk
4 oz. cherries
few drops vanilla essence

Cream the margarine and the sugar until very light and fluffy. Separate the eggs, adding the yolks to the fat and sugar, and whisking the whites until stiff. Add the sieved flour, salt and baking powder to the egg mixture alternately with the milk.

Fold in the cherries and vanilla essence, and lastly the whipped whites.

Bake in a loaf tin for about 1 hour. (375°F. — Gas Mark 5). This cherry cake improves with keeping.

Pearl's ginger cake

you will need	6 oz. margarine
	8 tablespoons golden syrup
	1½ teaspoons bicarbonate soda
	2 tablespoons milk
	2 tablespoons lemon juice
	2 eggs
	8 oz. self-raising flour
	½ teaspoon salt
	2 teaspoons ginger
	½ teaspoon cinnamon
	2 oz. sultanas, optional

Heat the fat and syrup gently in a large pan until the fat has melted, then bring quickly to the boil. Remove from the heat.

Stir in the bicarbonate of soda and beat with a wooden spoon for 2 minutes.

Stir in the milk and lemon, drop in the eggs and beat again. Finally stir in the sieved dry ingredients and sultanas, if used.

Bake in a very moderate oven (325°F. — Gas Mark 3) for 1½ hours.

This ginger cake gets nice and sticky after a few days.

Fruit loaf

you will need
  12 oz. plain flour
  pinch salt
  1½ level teaspoons baking powder
  1 level teaspoon bicarbonate soda
  2 oz. lard
  2 oz. margarine
  8 oz. sugar
  1 tablespoon lemon rind, grated
  rind 1 orange
  6 oz. sultanas
  6 oz. dates
  ½ pint milk

Sieve together the flour, salt, baking powder and bicarbonate of soda. Rub in the fats, stir in the sugar, lemon rind, grated orange rind and fruit, and mix with the milk.

Bake in a large loaf tin for 45 minutes in a fairly hot oven (400°F. – Gas Mark 6) and then for 1¼ hours in a moderate oven (350°F. – Gas Mark 4). Cover the fruit loaf with metal foil for the last 1¼ hours cooking time.

This loaf should be kept for a few days before being cut. It will taste very good after being kept in a tin for a week, even better after a fortnight.

Variation

The ingredients of this fruit loaf can be varied. For instance: instead of 6 oz. dates, use 2 oz. quartered glacé cherries, 2 oz. roughly chopped walnuts and 2 oz. chopped peel. Mix and cook as above.

Chocolate cake

you will need
4½ oz. granulated sugar
4½ oz. margarine
3 eggs
½ teaspoon vanilla essence
3 oz. self-raising flour
3½ oz. chocolate powder

Cream the sugar and margarine until white. Beat the eggs until just frothy and add to the creamed mixture with the vanilla essence.

Sieve the flour and chocolate powder and fold gradually into the mixture.

Cook in a greased and floured tin, 7-inches square for 45 minutes in a moderate oven. (350°F. — Gas Mark 4).

Keeps very well if iced with dark chocolate icing, see below.

Dark chocolate icing

you will need
8 oz. unsweetened chocolate
8 oz. icing sugar
2 tablespoons water

Break the chocolate into small pieces and melt over hot water.

When liquid stir in the sieved icing sugar and add the minimum amount of water to make the icing workable. Use immediately.

Loaf cake

Sieve together the flour, baking powder, salt, ginger and cinnamon. Cream the margarine and sugar and separate the eggs. Add the yolks to the creamed mixture and beat vigorously, then fold in the flour and the milk alternately. Beat the egg whites until stiff, fold into the mixture.

Bake for 45 minutes in a greased baking tin $2 \times 6 \times 8$ inches in a moderate oven. (350°F. – Gas Mark 4).

When cold, ice with the cocoa and icing sugar mixed with just enough warm water to handle.

Variation

For a moister loaf cake, and one with a genuine malty flavour use only 4 tablespoons of milk, 2 tablespoons golden syrup and 2 tablespoons malt, and 8 oz. instead of 7 oz. flour. This cake will take about 15 minutes longer to cook, and you may prefer not to ice it. After it has been kept for a while it is delicious sliced thinly and buttered.

Malt loaf

you will need
¼ pint milk
8 oz. self-raising flour
1 teaspoon bicarbonate soda
1 egg
3 tablespoons syrup
4 oz. dried fruit

Put the milk in a saucepan to warm but not boil. Sieve the flour and bicarbonate soda into a mixing bowl, add the beaten egg and then the warmed milk. Now warm the syrup and add that to the mixture. Lastly stir in the dried fruit. Bake for 1 hour in a slow oven (320°F. – Gas Mark 3).

Walnut tea bread

you will need
4 eggs
6 oz. castor sugar
4 oz. finely chopped walnuts
juice and rind 1 orange
4 oz. self-raising flour

Separate the eggs, putting the whites into a small bowl or jug, and the yolks, into a mixing bowl, with the sugar. Whisk the whites until very stiff. Then whisk the yolks and sugar until thick and light in colour. Add the walnuts, the finely grated orange rind and juice and stir well. Fold in the flour and then the egg whites.

Bake in a buttered and paper lined 7-inches square tin for 45 minutes. (350°F.—Gas Mark 4).

Date loaf

you will need   2 oz. dates
1 oz. sultanas
1 teaspoon bicarbonate soda
1 oz. butter
¼ pint boiling water
6 oz. sugar
1 egg
8 oz. plain flour
1 teaspoon baking powder

Put the dates, sultanas, bicarbonate of soda and butter in a basin, pour on the boiling water, stir well and allow to cool. Add the sugar and the beaten egg. Gradually stir in the flour, then beat well and add the baking powder.

Bake in a 1 lb. loaf tin, well greased, for 1½ hours in a moderate oven. (350°F. – Gas Mark 4).

Serve in buttered slices. Keeps well.

Sponge square

you will need   3 eggs
4 oz. sugar
1 tablespoon water or lemon juice
2 oz. plain flour
pinch salt

Separate the eggs and beat the whites until stiff enough to invert the bowl. Whisk together the yolks, sugar and water or lemon juice, until very light and creamy. Sieve the flour 3 times and fold into the egg yolk mixture, then carefully fold in the egg whites. Bake in an unbuttered 7-inch square tin for 25 – 30 minutes in a moderate oven. (350°F. – Gas Mark 4).

Apple tea bread

you will need
3 oz. margarine
6 oz. plain flour
¼ teaspoon bicarbonate soda
¼ teaspoon baking powder
½ teaspoon cinnamon
½ teaspoon ground ginger
3 oz. sugar
6 oz. mixed dried fruit
½ pint thick apple purée

Cream the margarine. Mix in the flour, bicarbonate, baking powder and spices with a fork until crumbly. Stir in the sugar and dried fruit. Add the apple purée and mix well.

Bake in a greased loaf tin for 30 minutes in a fairly hot oven (400°F. – Gas Mark 7) and then reduce the heat to warm for another hour. (325°F. – Gas Mark 3). Leave in the tin for 30 minutes before turning out.

Keep for 3 – 4 days before using. This tea bread will keep in a tin or other airtight container for a month or two.

Honey sponge

you will need
4 oz. margarine
4 oz. castor sugar
1 dessertspoon honey
2 eggs, unbeaten
5 oz. self-raising flour
½ level teaspoon baking powder
3 tablespoons milk

Put all the ingredients into a warmed bowl and beat well for 1 minute. Bake in a 7-inch square tin in a moderate oven for 35 – 40 minutes. (350°F. – Gas Mark 4).

Ice with Honey fudge icing, see page 246.

245

Honey fingers

you will need
3 oz. dried apricots
2 tablespoons honey
3 oz. margarine
4 oz. flour
1 level teaspoon baking powder
2 oz. brown sugar
12 level tablespoons rolled oats

Chop the apricots finely and place in a small basin. Warm the honey and pour $\frac{1}{2}$ on the apricots, mixing well and keeping in a warm place until required. Now add the margarine to the remainder of the honey and put on a gentle heat. When they are melted, stir in the sieved flour and baking powder, the sugar and the oats. Mix well.

Spread half the mixture over a $7\frac{1}{2}$-inch square greased baking tin, then spread the apricot and honey mixture over, and top with the rest of the oat mixture. Press down well.

Bake until golden brown, about 40 minutes, in a moderate oven. (350°F. – Gas Mark 4).

Cut into fingers when nearly cold.

Honey fudge icing

you will need
6 oz. icing sugar
2 oz. margarine
1 dessertspoon honey
1 dessertspoon lemon juice
1 dessertspoon water

Sift sugar into a bowl. Heat sliced margarine with other ingredients but do not allow to boil. Pour on to sugar and beat until smooth. Stir until required consistency, either for pouring for smooth icing or spreading for rough icing.

Honey cake

you will need
1 oz. mixed peel
1 oz. sultanas
orange juice
½ pint sour cream
1 egg
4 oz. soft brown sugar
9 oz. wholemeal flour
3 tablespoons honey, warmed
1 oz. chopped walnuts
1 good teaspoon baking powder, sieved

Soak the peel and sultanas in enough orange juice to cover for ½ hour. Whisk together the sour cream, egg and sugar. Fold in the flour, warmed honey, fruit and nuts. Mix very thoroughly, and then add the sieved baking powder, folding it in until thoroughly mixed.

Turn into a 2 lb. loaf tin, well greased, and cook for 1¾ hours at 300°F. – Gas Mark 3. This is a substantial rather sticky cake and improves with keeping.

Honey snaps

you will need
2 oz. butter
2 oz. castor sugar
2 level tablespoons clear honey
2 oz. plain flour
¼ teaspoon mixed spice
½ teaspoon ground ginger

Melt butter, sugar and honey in a pan. Remove from heat and stir in sieved flour and spices. Mix well. Drop in teaspoons well apart on greased baking sheet. Bake in oven 275°F. or Mark 4 – 5 until golden brown and bubbly. Cool slightly. Loosen with palette knife and roll quickly round greased spoon handle.

Shortbread

you will need   4 oz. good margarine
6 oz. plain flour
¼ level teaspoon salt
3 oz. castor sugar

Leave the margarine to soften at room temperature for and hour before using. Sieve the flour and salt together, stir in the sugar, and rub in the margarine. Press the mixture together until it forms a lump, and then break off a piece the size of an egg and roll between the palms until smooth and free from cracks. Repeat until all the mixture has been kneaded, then form it all into 1 large smooth ball and roll it out about ½-inch thick to fit a 7-inch sandwich tin. Flute the edges, prick all over, and mark into 8 sections with a knife. Tie a 3-inch strip of brown paper round the tin to prevent the shortbread from getting too brown.

Bake in a moderately hot oven for 40 minutes. (370°F.—Gas Mark 5).

Allow to cool slightly before cutting.

Viennese tartlets

you will need   4 oz. butter or margarine
1 oz. castor sugar
few drops vanilla essence
4 oz. plain flour
icing sugar
red jam

Beat fat and sugar together until very white and creamy. Add the vanilla essence. Blend in the flour.

Pipe circles of the mixture into paper cases, or spoon

it in and hollow the centre. Bake for 25 minutes in a moderate oven. (350°F. — Gas Mark 4).

When cool dredge with icing sugar and fill the centre with a little jam. These tartlets keep very well.

Oat flapjacks

you will need
6 oz. margarine
6 oz. brown sugar
8 oz. rolled oats
pinch salt

Melt the margarine over a low heat. Remove from the heat and stir in the sugar, oats and salt. Mix very well together, turn the mixture into a greased swiss roll tin and press down. Bake for 30 minutes in a moderate oven. (370°F. — Gas Mark 5).

Leave to cool for 5 minutes, then cut into fingers. Turn out of the tin when quite cold.

Oatcake

you will need
$3\frac{1}{2}$ oz. margarine
$3\frac{1}{2}$ oz. soft brown sugar
6 oz. rolled oats

Melt the margarine and brown sugar together in a saucepan. Stir in the rolled oats, mixing well. Turn into a greased 7-inch square tin and bake for 15 — 20 minutes in a moderate oven (350°F. — Gas Mark 4).

Mark into squares or oblongs while still warm and cut into pieces when cold.

Cheese straws

you will need
2 oz. plain flour
pinch salt
$\frac{1}{2}$ level teaspoon cayenne pepper
2 oz. margarine
3 oz. grated cheese
1 egg yolk

Sift the flour, salt and pepper together and rub in the margarine. Add the cheese and bind with the egg yolk, using a very little water if necessary.

Roll out to about $\frac{1}{8}$-inch thick and cut into narrow strips measuring about $\frac{1}{4} \times 4$ inches. Reserve some of the pastry to make rings of about 2-inch diameter in which to serve bundles of the cooked straws.

Bake on a greased tray for about 5 minutes in a hot oven. (450°F. – Gas Mark 8).

Index:

254